DBT

Therapeutic Activity Ideas for Kids and Caregivers

DBT

Therapeutic Activity Ideas for Kids and Caregivers

Carol Lozier, MSW LCSW

Illustrations created by Carol Lozier with the exceptions of several borders and lines created by Sonya DeHart design. Many thanks to Sonya for her clip art which can be found at her website: www.SonyaDehartDesign.com

Cover/Interior Design by the Book Cover Whisperer:
ProfessionalBookCoverDesign.com

ISBN: 978-0989881-53-1 Paperback
ISBN: 978-0989881-54-8 eBook

Printed in the U.S.A.

FIRST EDITION

Contents

Acknowledgments

First and foremost, all thanks to God, the giver of wisdom.

I would like to express love and gratitude to my family and friends for their ongoing love and support.

A special thank you to my life partner, John Coy, for his patience and support during this project.

Thank you to my best friend, sister, fellow DBTer, and proofreader, Lynn Waldman-Flax.

Thank you to my adult children, Rachel DeWitt and Aaron Lindner, who cheer me on and teach me about stocks, math, workouts, makeup, social media, Love Island, and life.

I want to express gratitude for my new grand babies, Lexi and Liam, who add so much sweetness and joy to our life!

Lastly, I want to thank the kids, teens, and caregivers in my DBT skills groups. I appreciate the contributions you all have made to the pages in this book. You all have brought these pages to life for so many others who are striving for a life worth living.

Introduction

Dialectical Behavior Therapy (DBT) is a cognitive behavioral therapy created by Dr. Marsha Linehan in the late 1980's to treat individuals diagnosed with borderline personality disorder and chronic suicidal thinking. DBT has also been shown to be an effective treatment for numerous disorders including depression, post traumatic stress disorder, and eating disorders (Linehan, 2015a, 2015b). In 2011, DBT was adapted and found to be effective in treating adolescents, age 12-18 (Rathus, 2015).

More recently, DBT has been modified for children, ages 6-12. DBT for children (DBT-C) continues to be researched and early studies show it may be helpful for children who struggle with intense emotions, disruptive behaviors, and challenging relationships (Perepletchikova 2011). Because emotionally dysregulated children often develop maladaptive coping skills in attempts to self regulate, DBT-C is designed to teach them new and more effective ways of coping.

There is a clear need for therapists and others to teach DBT-C to children early and in numerous settings in the community. Hopefully, these handouts and worksheets will make it feasible for therapists, school counselors, teachers, and others to include DBT-C as part of their therapy or curriculum. The handouts and worksheets are an invaluable tool for those who are new to the profession as well as those who have been in the field for many years.

Throughout the book the word "practitioner" or "therapist" will be used though it is understood that the provider could also be a social worker, counselor, psychologist, teacher, residential counselor, case manager, behavior trainer, mental health worker, skills trainer, or other DBT trainer. In addition, the term "caregiver" will be used throughout the book to represent all the different people and settings where children are raised such as, birth or step family, relatives, foster home or group home placement, and residential care.

CHILDREN AND CAREGIVERS LEARN DBT TOGETHER

For the child population, ages 6-12, the therapist works jointly with the child and caregiver in sessions. The caregiver's participation is crucial for the child to learn DBT skills in session, practice skills at home, and then implement the skills in their environment. Additionally, the caregiver helps the child with daily homework, practicing skills to be generalized to the child's life.

When a caregiver is present in the therapy room, they are able to observe and model the therapist's practice with the child as well as the delicate balance of validation and pushing for change. The caregiver learns the cadence of validation and change which increases the probability of practicing a similar balance in the home environment.

As caregivers learn and practice DBT skills alongside their child they are more likely to be skillful even in times of dysregulation. When a child is dysregualted the caregiver can be mindful and remain calm, and if the timing is right, model and encourage the child to behave skillfully too.

SCHOOL AGE DEVELOPMENT AND WORKING WITH CHILDREN

Elementary age kids are fun! They are inquisitive, say exceptionally humorous comments, and have amazing insight about themselves and others.

Over the last thirty years I have provided therapy to children and families in multiple settings including, therapeutic preschool, residential treatment center, outpatient community mental health center, parochial schools, and outpatient private practice. I would like to share some thoughts from my experience with this population.

1. Be yourself. Children are quick to notice insincerity; be genuine with them.

2. Engage children by being at their physical level. Sit on the floor with them or stoop down to maintain eye contact.

3. Do not have objects in the therapy room that are precious to you or can not be replaced. Children are often inquisitive of your belongings

and want to know about each item in the office. On occasion, through their curiosity or dysregulation things will get broken. As the therapist if something breaks you will need to remain calm and nonjudgmental.

4. You may have to refocus the child several times during the session. Bring their attention back to you through comments such as, "Ready?" "Look at me . . . " or "Eyes on me . . .".
5. Do not be afraid to ask them tough questions. Often, children understand themselves and their family dynamics even if they have not verbalized them in the past. Give the child an opportunity to express their opinion, and you will be amazed by their perceptive answers.
6. Show respect through mirroring their interpersonal cadence. For example, if the child is quiet use a quiet voice and mannerism.
7. Use multi-sensory learning. Each child has their own learning style, and therefore it is best to use all three styles as you teach concepts to them. The three learning styles are auditory, visual, and kinesthetic or learning by doing.

INTRODUCING DBT TO CHILDREN AND FAMILIES

Most children in this age range are open to meeting teachers and learning new information. Even if the practitioner is not a teacher in a school setting, the child will perceive them to be in a teaching role. Practitioners can use the following script to explain DBT to caregivers and children.

DBT has four groups of skills. The skills teach children to stay focused, keep their thoughts in the present moment instead of the past or future, stay in charge of their feelings, manage big feelings so they do not make their problems worse, and get along better with other people.

SKILL AQUISITION, STRENGTHENING, & GENERALIZATION

For each skill the child and caregiver will learn by three types of skill training (acquisition, strengthening, generalization) to fully integrate skilled behavior into the child and caregiver's lifestyle. In *skill acquisition*, the therapist teaches and models new material. This is accomplished through verbal explanation, discussion, practice, role plays, and modeling.

Then *skill strengthening* is used to fine-tune and increase the likelihood of the child or caregiver using the behaviors. The child and caregiver rehearse the behavior in the office or classroom, the practitioner provides feedback, and then positively reinforces their skillful behavior. Skill strengthening uses shaping, feedback, and behavioral rehearsal in session.

Finally, practitioners actively encourage the child and caregiver during *skill generalization* as they integrate skilled behavior through homework, diary card, phone coaching outside of session, and DBT skill apps. In this phase it is essential for the caregiver to create an environment where the child is encouraged and is reinforced to practice skilled behavior.

THE ACTIVITY BOOK

DBT Therapeutic Activity Ideas for Kids and Caregivers is a collection of handouts and worksheets for practitioners to use in individual sessions, small groups, or class rooms. The activity book is not a comprehensive DBT book rather it is meant to be supplemental to a DBT manual. The handouts and worksheets have been modified specifically for elementary age children while keeping in mind that they will also be receiving help from adults in their environment. The DBT skills are described to them with age appropriate vocabulary, fun fonts, and pictures.

Each sheet can be used as a stand alone activity or as a companion within a structured program. The skills are typically taught in sequence, but individual skills can be identified according to the child's need and used for teaching.

Each skill will first be explained to the child (and caregiver) along with a handout, and then followed with a worksheet for practice and/or homework. The handout explains the skill and its steps. After the explanation is a list of questions the practitioner can ask the child or caregiver to enhance discussion of the skill. These questions will be under the heading, "Discussion Questions," and are a guide for practitioners to lead the conversation. Practitioners can alter the questions to the child's developmental level using vocabulary that is familiar to the child. The worksheet can be used as practice during the counseling session, given as homework, or both. Though it may not be stated each time, it is assumed that the caregiver will assist the child with their weekly homework.

In addition, some of the younger children in this age group are still learning to read, and many may not even read "chapter books" yet. Therefore, some of the children may need more help than others in reading and understanding some of the words on the sheets. Much of the DBT language will be new to the child and caregiver. As you encounter each new word, define it using vocabulary that is familiar to the child and caregiver yet still incorporating DBT language. Each time, remind the child of the word's meaning until the child remembers it. Then, when you come across the word, pause and allow the child to define it. Positively reinforce the child's efforts to define the word; refine their understanding of the word if it is not accurate. Continue to teach the child and caregiver proper terms using DBT language. Over time, the child will gain a DBT vocabulary and be able to use it correctly.

DBT has been researched and modified for the child population since 2011 (Pereplechikova, 2011). All of the activity book's DBT-C skills are based on Dr. Linehan's (2015a, 2015b) original work unless otherwise specified. Some of the DBT-C skills in the activity book have been adapted from their original design to transform an abstract concept into a more concrete one.

We will be covering all four modules as well as a couple concepts from the module, walking the middle path, which was an addition in the *DBT Skills Manual for Adolescents* (Rathus, 2015).

In agreement with my previous book, *DBT Therapeutic Activity Ideas for Working with Teens* (Lozier, 2018), this book will also indicate the module of each skill by a circled initial in the upper right or left corner of the sheet. The initials will be:

Mindfulness = mi
Distress tolerance = dt
Emotion regulation = er
Interpersonal effectiveness = ie

The last section of the activity book is specifically for caregivers. This section will discuss concepts within the behavior change and acceptance strategies including behavior modification, validation, wise minded parenting, and relational mindfulness.

ADHERENT VS. INFORMED DBT

A comprehensive or adherent DBT-C program contains: individual therapy, group skills training, phone coaching with caregivers, caregiver training, and therapist-team consultation. Unfortunately, some therapists do not have a team or all components of a comprehensive DBT program. They can still teach DBT skills to kids in their practice or program, and this is referred to as DBT informed therapy.

Since my last book, I have completed a sixteen month Intensive Plus DBT Program. It has been an amazing experience learning from top trainers in Behavior Tech's training program as well as my worldwide consultation team representing the countries of New Zealand, Australia, and Canada. I am hopeful that my expanded knowledge will be reflected on the pages of this book, and in turn, will better equip the reader in their own practice or program. After all, we all have the same goal—to help kids and families have a life worth living!

SECTION 1

What is DBT for Children?

Dialectical Behavior Therapy (DBT) is a cognitive behavioral therapy created by Dr. Marsha Linehan in the late 1980's to treat individuals diagnosed with borderline personality disorder and chronic suicidal thinking. DBT has also been shown to be an effective treatment for numerous disorders including depression, post traumatic stress disorder, and eating disorders (Linehan, 2015a, 2015b).

More recently, DBT has been modified for children, ages 6-12. DBT for children (DBT-C) continues to be researched and studies show it may be helpful for children who struggle with intense emotions, disruptive behaviors, and challenging relationships (Perepletchikova, 2011). Because emotionally dysregulated children often develop maladaptive coping skills in attempts to self regulate, DBT-C is designed to teach them new and more effective ways of coping.

> "Kids learn DBT skills in various settings including individual, group, residential, and in the classroom."

Kids learn DBT skills in various settings including individual, group, residential, and in the classroom. The child is assigned weekly homework, and practices skills on a daily basis with their caregiver. The practitioner can teach the skills in the sequence outlined in the book or they can teach the skills based on the child's individual need.

DBT is composed of four groups of skills or modules: mindfulness, distress tolerance, emotion regulation, and interpersonal effectiveness. Within each module, there are numerous skills for children to learn and use in order to create a balanced life. It is imperative that caregivers also delve into learning DBT to ensure the child has the opportunity to generalize skills into their everyday life.

1. THE FOUR MODULES

1. Mindfulness

In DBT, mindfulness is named "core mindfulness" as it is the foundation within each skill. Mindfulness is paying attention in the moment without judgment of oneself or others. It is purposefully paying attention to our thoughts, feelings, body sensations; and externally to our environment using the five senses of sight, sound, touch, taste and smell. Mindfulness is most effective when kids and their caregivers maintain a consistent practice. A routine practice improves their ability to focus, and it increases feelings of happiness. In DBT, mindfulness is composed of two parts, the WHAT and HOW skills. The WHAT skills consist of observe, describe, and participate; the HOW skills include nonjudgmental, one-mindful, and effective. In the activity book, they will also learn to manage distractions during mindfulness and anchor themselves in the moment.

"Mindfulness is most effective when kids and their caregivers maintain a consistent practice."

2. Distress Tolerance

In the distress tolerance module, kids learn skills to tolerate and survive emotional crises without making the situation worse through impulsive reactions. The impulsive behaviors a practitioner may witness or hear from children include yelling, cussing, throwing things, refusing to talk, or avoiding eye contact.

Distress tolerance skills are divided into two groups: crisis survival and reality acceptance. Crisis survival skills help the child to problem solve, and to manage a painful situation without making it worse. The reality acceptance skills give children the ability to accept a situation as it is without trying to change it or fight against it.

3. Emotion Regulation

Emotion regulation skills increase a child's ability to control their emotions or to be more capable of managing them. In this module the child learns to understand and name emotions, to change their emotional response, to reduce their vulnerability to emotion mind, and to manage difficult emotions. Emotion regulation skills improve a child's self-awareness by knowing their emotion and the corresponding cues of body sensation, tone of voice, and facial expression. The skills also teach kids to build positive experiences and emotions so that they can be less sensitive to painful emotions.

"Emotion regulation skills help the child to manage negative and overwhelming emotions, and to increase positive emotions."

4. Interpersonal Effectiveness

The interpersonal effectiveness skills help children to maintain relationships and get along better with others. These relationships can be with various people including parents, foster family, siblings, relatives, teachers, coaches, peers, neighbors, and acquaintances. This module of DBT skills teach kids to maintain relationships, get their needs met in an effective way, and maintain self-respect.

Additionally, the kids will learn to repair wrongdoing or mistakes with others, to say no to unwanted requests, to express their feelings and opinions effectively, and to encourage themselves during overwhelming situations.

Handout Directions

Use the handout to describe the four modules of DBT to the child and caregiver. Explain each module using the above information as well as additional sources (see References page), and list a few of the skills in each module.

Discussion Questions

- Which module or group of skills do you feel will be most helpful to you or your child?
- Which module or group of skills do you already use most successfully?

What Is DBT?

4 Modules or Groups of skills

Mindfulness

* Keep your focus on the moment
* Be less judgmental
* Be self-aware of feelings, thoughts and body sensations
* Notice what's around you with 5 senses
* Live effectively- let go of being "right" and things being "fair"

Distress Tolerance

* Go through and survive very challenging emotions without making things worse
* Accept and go through situations in life that you may not like
* Tolerate painful events and emotions that can't be changed right away

Emotion Regulation

* Increase self control of emotions
* Understand emotions more
* Be able to name emotions
* Change unwanted emotions
* Lessen the likelihood of tipping to emotion mind
* Be in charge of difficult emotions

Interpersonal Effectiveness

* Keep relationships
* Improve relationships
* Learn to deal with disagreements
* Get needs met from others
* Say "no" when you need to
* Keep self respect in relationships
* Repair wrongdoing or mistakes in relationships

Adapted from Linehan, *DBT Skills Training Manual* (2015b)

Worksheet Directions

This worksheet can be given as homework or in session to further fine tune the child and caregiver's understanding of the four modules. On a whiteboard, write the name of each module, and describe the goals within each of the four modules. In a group setting, encourage members to identify the goals within each module.

Suggestions for the Therapist

This is one of the first homework assignments in the activity book. Therefore, be sure to positively reinforce the child and caregiver's efforts. As they describe the goals of each module, reinforce their attempts to explain the goals.

What Is DBT?
4 Modules or Groups of skills

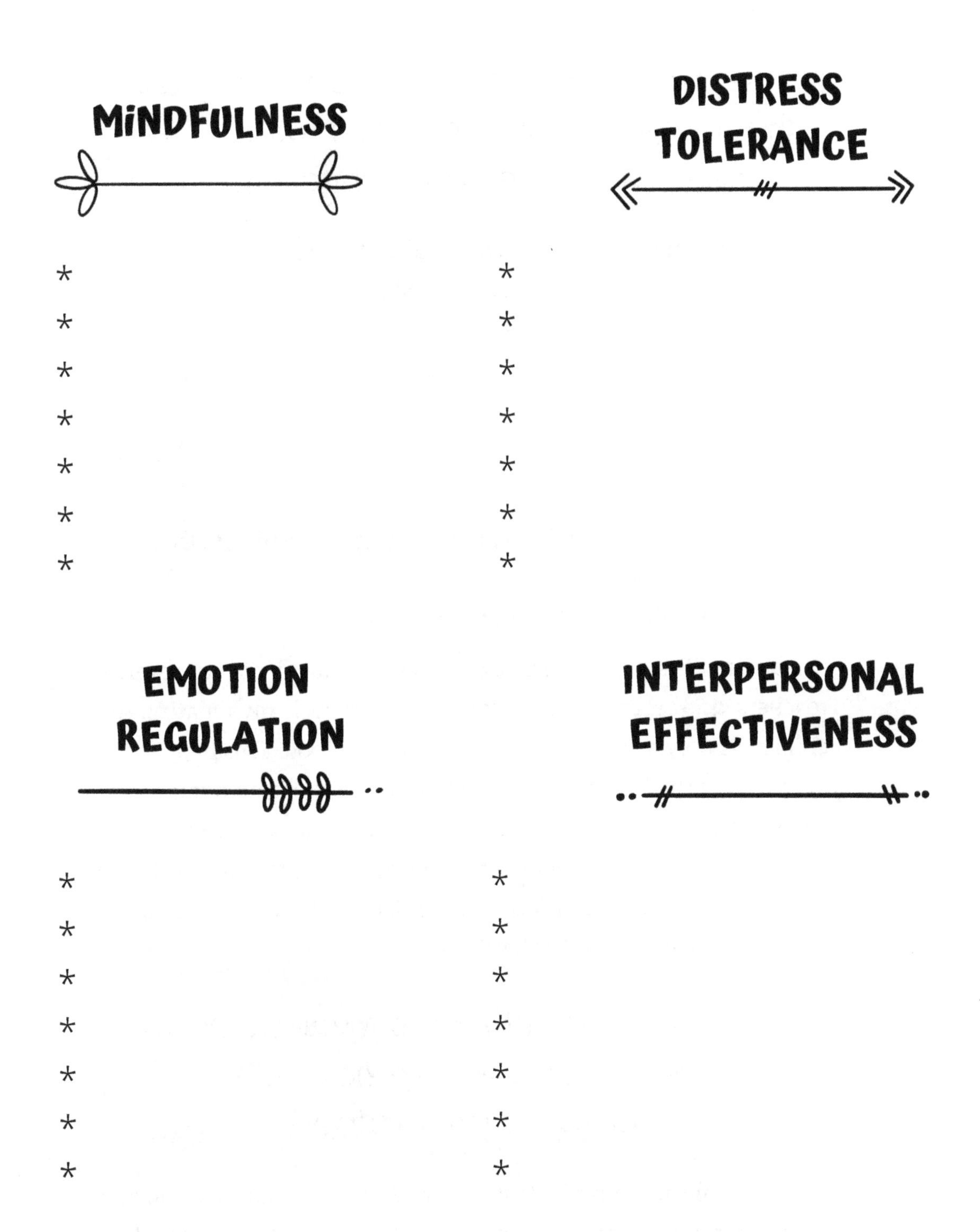

Adapted from Linehan, *DBT Skills Training Manual* (2015b)

2. BIOSOCIAL THEORY

Biosocial theory was developed by Dr. Marsha Linehan (Linehan, 2015b). Over a period of time, when an emotionally sensitive child is in an invalidating environment it leads to difficulties in their emotion regulation.

"The 'bio' in biosocial refers to the idea that some people are born with a pre-disposition to emotional sensitivity."

The "bio" in biosocial refers to the idea that some people are born with a predisposition to emotional sensitivity. Emotional sensitivity is shown in the following ways:

Emotionally sensitive- experience emotion more often than others.
Emotionally reactive- feel emotions more intensely and have strong reactions.
Slow return to baseline- have difficulty returning to their own level of calm . . .
which is different for each individual.

"Social" signifies the child's caregiving environment such as parents, teachers, and relatives. When an environment is invalidating the child feels they are not being heard or understood. This happens in several ways including an invalidation of the child's emotions (their emotions are wrong or bad), the child's emotional expression is punished ("You're too old to act like that!") or the caregiver conveys to the child an oversimplified approach to problem solving ("You're gonna have to toughen up; just try harder").

"When an environment is invalidating the child feels they are not being heard or understood."

Biosocial theory is illustrated in the transactional relationship between the child and their caregiver. The transaction begins when the child attempts to communicate their feelings. If it is not received well, the child feels invalidated, and as a result their behavior escalates (exaggeration, yelling, cussing) as they are feeling more vulnerable. Then the caregiver, oftentimes unknowingly, increases the invalidation ("What is your problem?"). The transaction continues as they influence one another; the child feeling more invalidated and thus vulnerable, and the caregiver responding with more invalidation.

The point of discussing this transactional pattern is not to blame caregivers rather to help them understand the transaction, to identify their part, and instead to wisely respond with validation.

Handout Directions

Explain biosocial theory to the children and caregivers. Most people respond to the information with relief, and are pleased to hear they are not alone in their experience or their child's experience of emotional sensitivity.

Discussion Questions

- Do you experience any of the three emotional sensitivities? Or for caregivers, do any of the three emotional sensitives describe their child?
- Do you agree that people are biologically predisposed to emotional sensitivity? Explain your answer.
- Do you (child or caregiver) experience invalidation at home, school, a relative's home, work, or other places in the community?
- Do you notice an invalidating transaction in any of the relationships in your life? Describe it.

What Is DBT?

Biosocial Theory

Biosocial theory says that over time emotionally sensitive kids, who are raised in an invalidating environment, have a harder time staying in charge of their emotions. Let's explore the meaning of biosocial theory:

BIO refers to your biological makeup. Some kid's brains are wired to be more emotional than others; these kids are referred to as emotionally sensitive. Their emotional sensitivity can be seen in several ways:

1. Emotional sensitivity - feeling upset or bothered more easily than others.

2. Emotional reactivity - feeling emotions intensely and have strong reactions.

3. Slow to baseline - have a harder time returning to their own level of self-control and calm.

SOCIAL refers to a child's social environment. In other words, the people around them: family, friends, teachers, and so on. When a child feels as though these people listen and understand their feelings and behavior it is validating.
On the other hand, invalidation is not feeling heard or understood by others. Invalidation makes a child feel confused and unsure if they can trust their own feelings.
When people invalidate a child they may say comments such as, "That's ridiculous," "You're a drama queen," or they may roll their eyes or ignore them. Invalidation, whether it's intentional or not, is hurtful.

Adapted from Linehan, *DBT Skills Training Manual* (2015b)

Worksheet Directions

This worksheet is to be completed in session as it can bring up high emotions while addressing the child's invalidating environment. Together, look at the three emotional sensitivities; read them aloud with the child. Prompt the child to check the ones that pertain to him or her. As you review each one, allow the child to express how each one describes him or her. Caregivers can add additional information as well.

Next, look at the list under the title, invalidating environment. Read this list too, and allow the child to explain how each of these describes his or her current or past environment. If they have an additional example, encourage the child to add it next to the "Other" option. Again, allow the caregiver to add any information.

Suggestions for the Therapist

As you discuss this sheet, be prepared that caregivers may blame themselves or others for having been invalidating to the child. Remind them this is not about blame, instead it is a way to understand the transaction, and to create new and more effective interactions with the child.

The child may also bring up other invalidating situations with peers or siblings. Allow them to share any information, validate their experience, and positively reinforce their willingness to discuss it with you or their caregiver.

What Is DBT?

Biosocial Theory

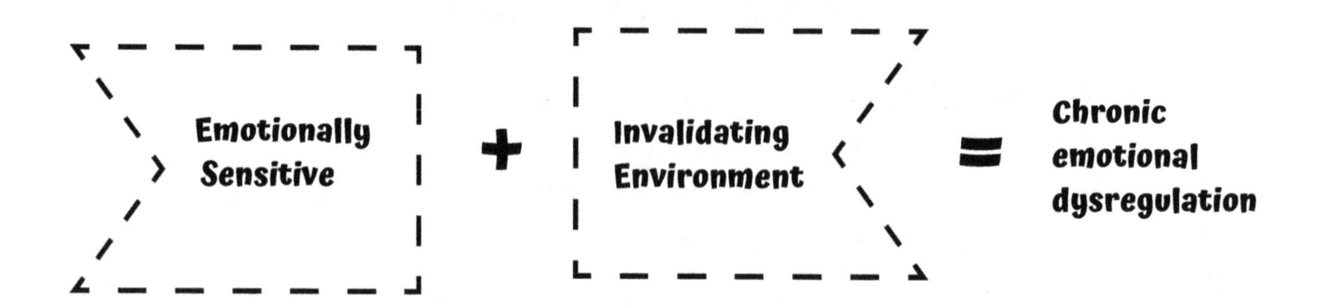

Check the ones that apply to you and your social environment:

EMOTIONALLY SENSITIVE

Emotional Sensitivity:
__Things seem to bother or upset me easily.

Emotional Reactivity:
__I tend to feel my emotions intensely with strong reactions.

Slow to Baseline:
__It takes me a while to calm down and have more self-control.

INVALIDATING ENVIRONMENT

__I have people in my life (now or in the past) who don't understand or hear my emotions or thoughts.

Verbal Invalidation:
__"You're over reacting."
__"Don't be so silly!"
__Mock me
__Others:

Nonverbal Invalidation:
__Ignore me
__Eye rolling
__Others:

Adapted from Linehan, *DBT Skills Training Manual* (2015b)

3. DBT ACRONYMS

When children are dysregulated, in emotion or behavior, it is also difficult for them to have clear thoughts. Therefore, a number of DBT skills use acronyms or mnemonics to help kids remember the skills in times of distress. Though it may be tempting to skip the handout, it is important as acronyms are included in numerous DBT skills.

Note: There is only a worksheet for this skill.

Worksheet Directions

Clarify the definition of an acronym—a word formed from the initial letters of other words, and the recognition that they are a significant part of DBT. Discuss the value of an acronym occurs when the child's emotion goes up, their "brain power" goes down. As a result, they are not able to think clearly and rationally as they are in emotion mind.

On this worksheet kids can choose the word "school" or "hobbies" to describe the acronym. If the child prefers, they can choose a different word. Likewise, the practitioner may choose another word that is more pertinent to the child's situation or environment.

This worksheet can also be completed as a group activity. In this instance, write the chosen word on a white board, and invite all the children, or the child and caregiver, to offer words that correspond to each letter in the word. Remember to positively reinforce their participation.

Discussion Questions

- Can you think of a time when you were upset, and could not think clearly? Describe what happened. (This question can be posed to both children and caregivers.)

What Is DBT?
Acronyms

An acronym is a word created by the first letters of other words. In DBT, acronyms help you to remember skills to use in upsetting moments. Let's practice making acronyms of your own.
Following the equal sign, write words to describe your thoughts about "school" OR "hobbies" to create the acronyms below.

S =
C =
H=
O=
O=
L=

H=
O=
B=
B=
I=
E=
S=

Adapted from Linehan, *DBT Skills Training Manual* (2015b)

4. DIALECTICS

Dialectics is the "D" in DBT, and a central concept in the therapy. Many of the abstract principles in a dialectical worldview are challenging for children to understand. In the activity book, the focus will remain on the idea of tolerating the co-existence of two opposing points of views. Two things that seem to be opposite can both be true, and they can both be held at the same time. These opposites points of view both have important pieces of truth to contribute at the same time.

"Two things that seem to be opposite can both be true, and they can both be held at the same time."

When children get stuck in a polarization (an extreme position or absolute truth), they are missing the other person's point of view. In a polarization the child may take a strong position and think "I'm right" and others are "wrong." When children consider others point of view, they blend the two sides together which allows them to get unstuck and move forward with the other person.

"When children consider others point of view, they blend the two sides together which allows them to get unstuck . . ."

Some extreme words you may hear from a child when they are stuck in a polarization include:

"always" or "never"
"right" or "wrong"
"should" or "shouldn't"
"fair" or "unfair"
"either" or "or"

"You should . . ."
"You are . . . "
"It's not fair at all that . . ."
"You make me . . ."

Handout Directions

Teach the child and caregiver, or children the dialectical concept of tolerating the co-existence of opposites. Begin by discussing opposites, and ask them to provide examples, such as up/down, empty/full, and so on.

Explain that polarized thoughts lay on the opposite end just like the opposite ends on a line; refer to the balance image on the handout. I also open my arms apart to show the child another image of opposite ends. Next, discuss the list of polarized thoughts on the handout including the question, "What are some polarized thoughts you have thought or said before?"

Lastly, teach the steps or dialectical equation that creates a dialectical, balanced thought from polarized thoughts. Let the children know they do not have to like or agree with the piece of truth.

Discussion Questions

- Can you name several opposites?
- Why do you think kids get stuck in a polarized thought like "You hate me!" or "It's not fair that I have to put away everyone's dishes."
- How do kids feel when they get stuck in a polarized thought?
- How do kids feel when they get unstuck, and can think dialectically?

Dialectical Thinking

What is DBT?

Polarized or opposite thoughts make kids "stuck," and cause problems in their life. A few examples of polarizations are when kids have thoughts with words like: either/or, always/never, should/shouldn't. Let's remember, it's important to consider the other person's side too. After all, there may be something you are missing!

Polarized thoughts

A few examples of polarized thoughts are:
"You always play with everyone else."
"You're the worst mom/dad ever."
"You never let me go to roller skating with my friends."
What are some polarized thoughts you have thought or said before?

Turn your polarized thought into a balanced thought by blending the two sides or polarized thoughts together. Use these steps to make a balanced (or dialectical) statement:

1. Notice your polarized thought or comment.
2. Identify the opposite thought or comment.
3. Find the piece of truth from each thought; put an "AND" in the middle. (Piece of truth + AND + Piece of truth.)
4. Mindfully say your balanced or dialectical thought.

Adapted from Linehan, *DBT Skills Training Manual* (2015b)

Worksheet Directions

The dialectical thinking skill has two worksheets, one is blank and the other one is completed. Give a completed worksheet to the child and caregiver, and review this worksheet using the vignette below.

Vignette: Janelle is 9 years old and is coming to the table for dinner before they run off to gymnastics class. At the dinner table, she sees that her mom made peanut butter sandwiches. Janelle feels very angry, and yells at her mom, "This is the worst day of my life!" Once calm, Janelle and her mom identify this is a polarized thought and together they create a dialectical thought.

As reflected in the completed worksheet, they first identify the opposite thought—"This is the best day of my life."

Secondly, they find the piece of truth in each statement.

Next, they add an "AND" in the middle of the two statements.

Finally, Janelle says the dialectical statement aloud.

Now, provide a blank worksheet to the child. The worksheet can be completed together in session with an example, or given as a homework assignment to change one polarized thought into a dialectical one.

Suggestions for the Therapist

An equation is a strategy to teach kids how to turn polarized thoughts into a dialectical thought. Write the equation on a white board, and allow the child to follow along as you demonstrate with an example or two.

Dialectical Thinking

What is DBT?

DIALECTICAL EQUATION:

1. Notice your polarized thought or comment.
2. Identify the opposite thought or comment.
3. Find the piece of truth from each thought; put an "AND" in the middle. (Piece of truth + AND + Piece of truth.)
4. Mindfully say your balanced or dialectical thought.

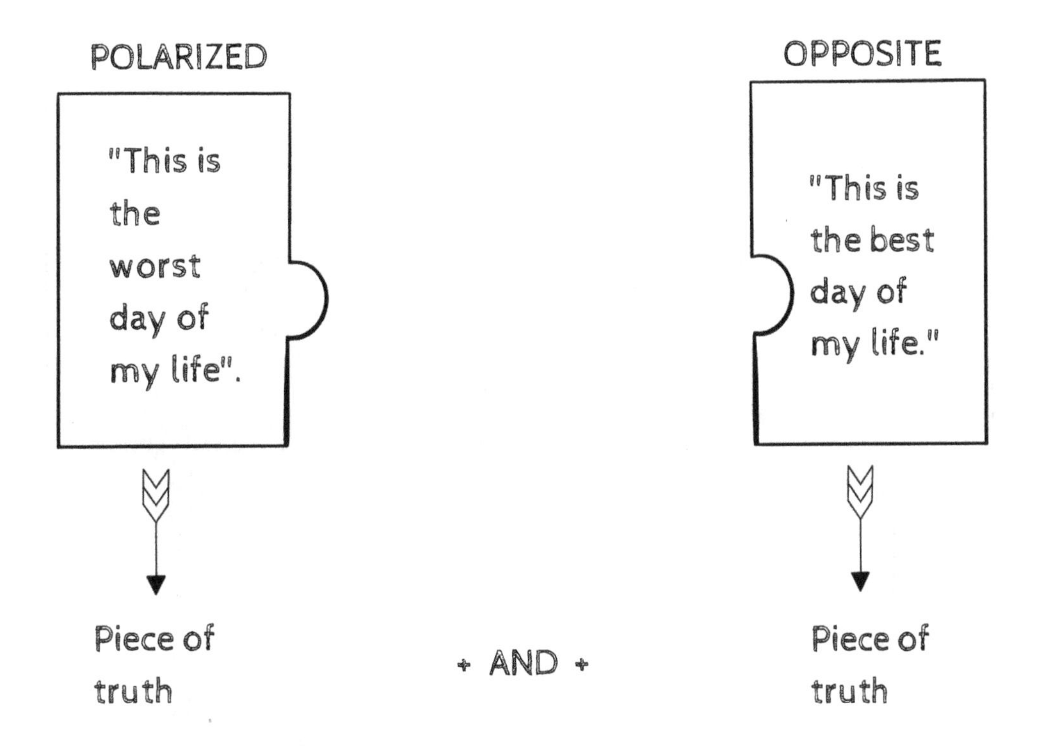

BALANCED OR DIALECTICAL

"I don't like to eat peanut butter sandwiches at dinner AND I like it when we eat mac and cheese.""

Adapted from Linehan, *DBT Skills Training Manual* (2015b)

Dialectical Thinking

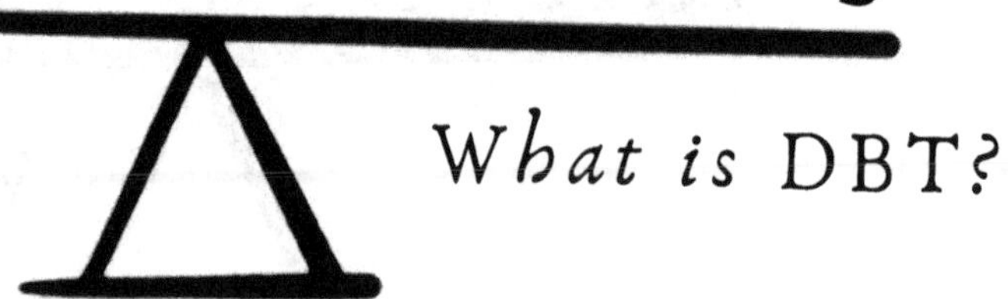

DIALECTICAL EQUATION:

1. Notice your polarized thought or comment.
2. Identify the opposite thought or comment.
3. Find the piece of truth from each thought; put an "AND" in the middle. (Piece of truth + AND + Piece of truth.)
4. Mindfully say your balanced or dialectical thought.

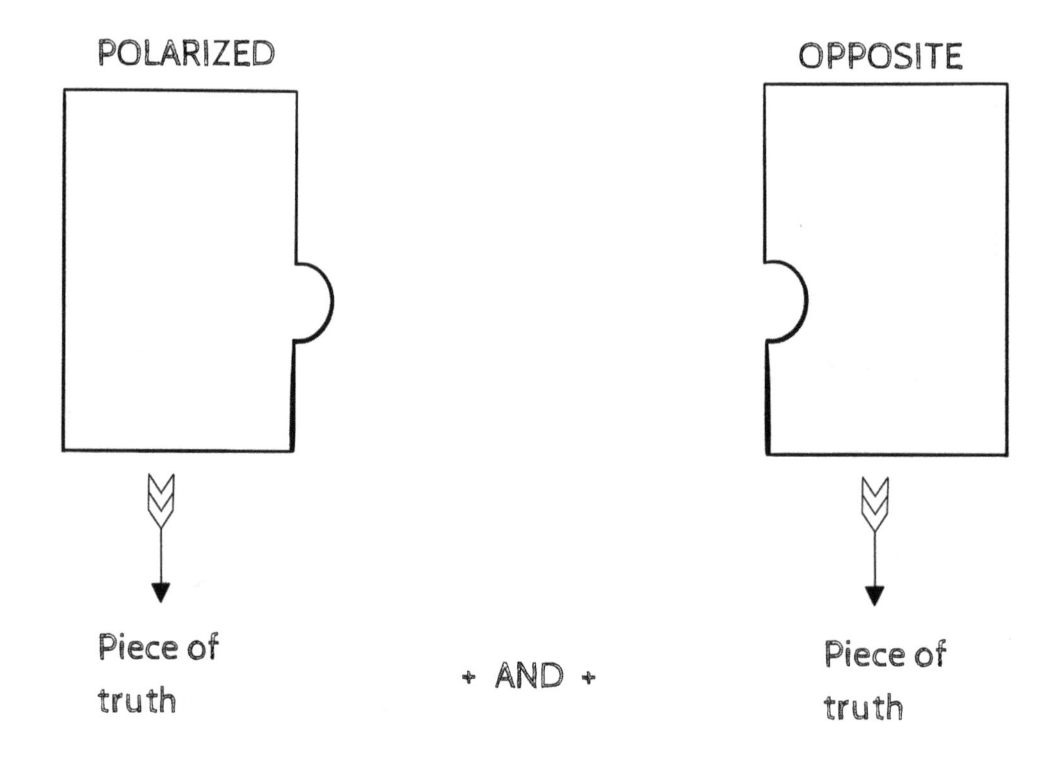

BALANCED OR DIALECTICAL

Adapted from Linehan, *DBT Skills Training Manual* (2015b)

5. VALIDATION

Validation is included in the section "What is DBT?" in the activity book. Validation is communicating to another person that you are listening and understand them, and that their feelings, thoughts, and actions make sense in the situation. Validation is not just agreeing with whatever the child is saying or doing, it requires you to find the piece of truth in their viewpoint. In DBT there are six levels of validation, and they include the following six levels.

1. Pay attention. Listen to the child; give them your full attention with eye contact. Ask questions and do not interrupt.
2. Accurate Reflection or Mirroring. Reflect back what you are hearing and understanding. Do not just parrot their words, instead summarize what you heard them say.
3. Reading Minds. Take the child's unspoken emotion, thought, or behavior and put it into words. Notice the child's body language, tone of voice, facial expression, and posture to figure out what might be happening in that moment. *Remember to check in and make sure your guess is accurate; ask, "Is that correct?"*
4. Validate in Terms of Past History. Connect current emotional reactions to past learning; communicate that you understand their reaction based on previous causes.
5. Validate in Terms of Present Situation. Acknowledge the person's feeling, thought, or action as reasonable in the situation. "Anybody would feel that way… "
6. Show Radical Genuineness. Treat them with respect and warmth, and as someone you care about. Do not treat the other person as incompetent or fragile.

Self Validation: All six levels of validation can be used for yourself too. Pay attention to your own thoughts, feelings, and behaviors; reflect back and describe them to yourself. Be aware and sensitive of what you need in situations. Attempt to understand your innermost thoughts and feelings and their cause; treat yourself with respect and warmth.

Invalidation: On the other hand, invalidation communicates to a child that their thoughts, feelings, or actions make no sense and are not worthy of your interest or time. Invalidation may or may not be intentional, but either way it is hurtful to children.

Handout Directions

Teach the child and caregiver the concepts of validation, self-validation, and invalidation. Connect these ideas back to biosocial theory, and the role invalidation plays in emotionally sensitive kids developing chronic emotional dysregulation. Point out the images on the page and discuss how they reflect the concepts. Validation causes positive thoughts and feelings while invalidation causes unwanted thoughts and feelings.

Discussion Questions

- Give examples of validation, self-validation, and invalidation.
- How do you feel when someone is validating versus invalidating to you?
- Who do you invalidate more: yourself or others?
- Name a situation and make a plan to cope ahead with self-validation.

For Caregivers:

- Which level of validation to you use most to validate your child?
- Which level of validation do you want to increase using with your child?

Validation & Invalidation

What is DBT?

Write 1 validating sentence, and 1 sentence of self-validation. Remember, no judging!

VALIDATION:

SELF-VALIDATION:

Write a few examples of invalidating words or behaviors.

INVALIDATION:

Adapted from Linehan, *DBT Skills Training Manual* (2015b)

Worksheet Directions

Instruct the children, with help from their caregiver, to write one example of validation and self-validation. Also, ask them to write examples of non-verbal and verbal invalidation.

Suggestions for the Therapist

As children discuss invalidation, pay close attention to any disclosures of traumatic invalidation and to those who have been formally diagnosed with PTSD.

Validation & Invalidation

What is DBT?

Write 1 validating sentence, and 1 sentence of self-validation. Remember, no judging!

VALIDATION:

SELF-VALIDATION:

Write a few examples of invalidating words or behaviors.

INVALIDATION:

Adapted from Linehan, *DBT Skills Training Manual* (2015b)

SECTION 2

Mindfulness

Mindfulness is noticing the present moment, on purpose, in a nonjudgmental way; it is paying attention to yourself internally (feelings, thoughts, body sensations) and externally with your five senses (sight, sound, taste, touch, smell).

In DBT, mindfulness is the first group of skills to learn; they are referred to as "core mindfulness" skills because they are the foundation of each skill. When an individual is mindfully using a skill they are in the moment, and paying full attention to their experience without judging themselves or others.

"Mindfulness is noticing the present moment, on purpose, in a nonjudgmental way . . ."

The mindfulness practice is a brief and fun, nonreligious experience with the goal of enhancing the child's focus, slowing their reactions to gain more self-control, and to increase their self-awareness. Mindfulness for kids is typically 1-5 minutes in length, and starts with simple activities to increase the child's success. Children begin mindfulness with concrete objects or self in the environment, progressing to mindfulness of the body, and then being mindful of the thinking process. (Hooker, 2008).

In DBT, mindfulness has two parts: WHAT skills and HOW skills. They will both be discussed in this section as well as three states of mind, anchoring, and three ways to practice mindfulness including coloring sheets.

1. THREE STATES OF MIND

Three states of mind is comprised of emotion mind, reasonable or thinking mind, and wise mind. Emotion mind is "hot," and ruled by feelings and urges. When a person is in emotion mind it is difficult for them to think logically, and their thoughts are heavily influenced by their current emotion. Reasonable mind is "cool," and ruled by facts, logic, and reason. In reasonable mind, the person ignores emotion and empathy, and would prefer to be practical when problem solving.

"Reasonable mind is "cool," and ruled by facts, logic, and reason."

Wise mind is the synthesis of both reason and emotion; it is the wisdom and intuition within each person. In wise mind, the person can blend opposites, and is willing to accept reality even when they do not like it or agree with it.

Note: There is only a handout for this skill.

Handout Directions

Explain emotion mind, reasonable mind, and wise mind; discuss examples in each state of mind. Some examples are:

> *Emotion mind*- excessive worry, avoid people or situations, yell. Walk out of class because someone is sitting in your seat.
> *Reasonable mind*- use logic to solve a problem, move forward from an argument without first resolving hurt feelings, avoid speaking up for yourself because "I'm not that important."
> *Wise mind*- Choose not to argue about a small issue because the relationship is more important, feel scared to ask your teacher about a grading mistake and asking anyway, do homework when you'd rather go outside to play.

Discussion Questions

- Do you get stuck more often in emotion mind or reasonable mind?
- What you do or think in each state of mind?
- Which emotions keep you from acting wisely?
- What are the benefits of both reason and emotion?
- Everyone has a wise mind. Do you agree? Explain your answer.
- Define intuition.

Three States of Mind

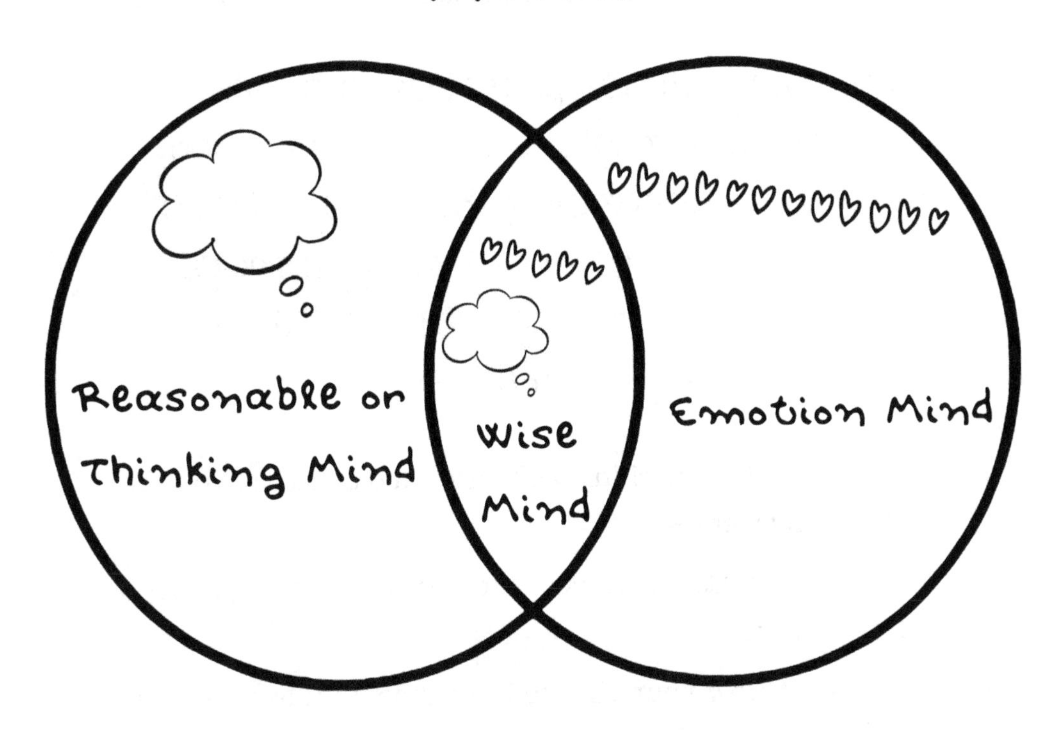

Reasonable or Thinking Mind	Wise Mind	Emotion Mind
Cool Facts Thinking Problem solving Thinking without considering emotion	Intuition Balancing both emotion and reason Clear thinking even when emotional	Hot Feelings Passion When emotions take over and facts are unimportant

Adapted from Linehan, *DBT Skills Training Manual* (2015b)

2. WHAT SKILLS

The WHAT skills are what you do to practice mindfulness. The three skills are done one at a time and include observe, describe, and participate. The WHAT skills help kids be in the moment, and be aware of themselves and the environment. Let's look at each of the three skills.

"The mindfulness practice is a brief and fun, nonreligious experience with the goal of enhancing the child's focus, slowing their reactions to gain more self-control, and to increase their self-awareness."

- Observe- wordless watching both inside and outside of yourself, using your five senses.
- Describe- put words to what you observed without interpretation; stick to the facts.
- Participate- throw yourself into the moment; fully experience whatever you are doing without being self-conscious.

Handout Directions

Incorporate all learning styles when you teach the WHAT skills to kids and caregivers. Verbally explain the skills, point out the visual images on the page to help them recall the three skills, and finally, practice the WHAT skills with them.

As previously stated, it is best for children to start a mindfulness practice with awareness of an objects such as candy, leaves, flowers, acorns, pinecones, shells, feathers, or other items from nature; music; outside sounds; cotton balls and many others—be creative! Once the child is more aware of their environment, move the practice to awareness of self, the child's body and behavior. For example, notice the coolness of breath as it enters the nose, and its warmth as it exhales out of the mouth. Next, the child is ready to pay attention to the thinking process; for example, notice thoughts and allow them to float away, or bring the mind back to the moment when it is distracted.

Now, let's practice mindfulness with awareness of an object in the environment. Choose an object and hand it to the child and caregiver. Ask them to notice the object and all of its details with their five senses. Allow the child and caregiver to notice the object for a minute or two; ask them to set it aside and use their words to describe the item. As they describe the object, the practitioner reinforces their description and also models describing the item back to them.

Discussion Questions

- When you participate, what are some thoughts or feelings that might hold you back from throwing yourself into the experience?
- Describe is putting words to an experience without interpretation. In the following sentences, identify the one that is describe and the one that is interpretation. 1. My sister's so mean and she hates me. 2. My sister is stomping her foot, and yelling, "Get out of my room now!"

Mindfulness Skills

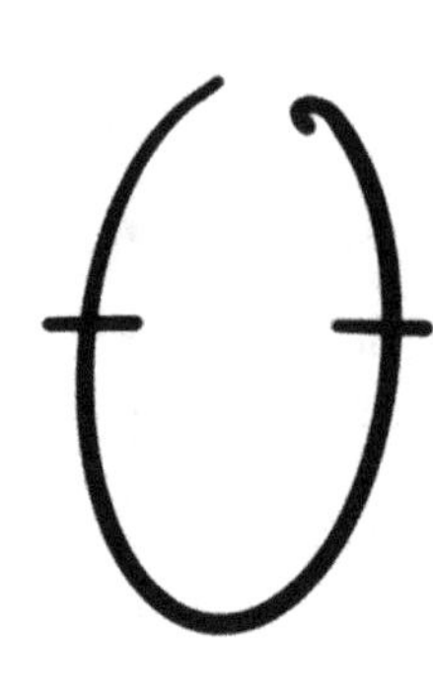

OBSERVE

Observe is also called, "Wordless watching." It is noticing or paying attention to the current moment, using your five senses. Be sure to notice both inside and outside of yourself.

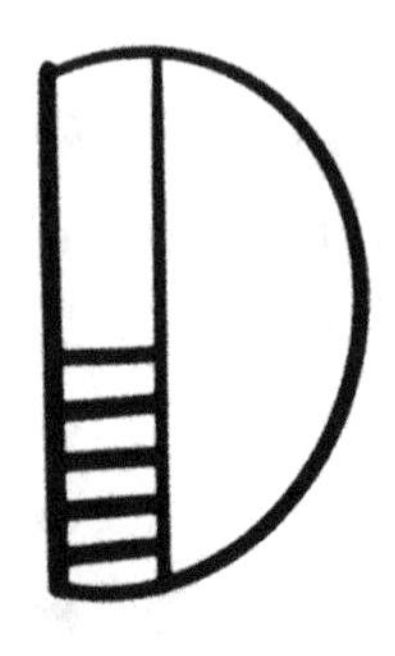

DESCRIBE

Describe is putting words to your experience. Remember to describe using facts, and not your interpretation (making up your own explanation) of the situation.

PARTICIPATE

Participate is being fully in the experience . . . don't hold back! Some people call this being "in the zone."

Adapted from Linehan, *DBT Skills Training Manual* (2015b)

Worksheet Directions

This worksheet can be given for homework, or used in session for practice. There are one to two examples provided under each skill. Instruct the kids and caregivers to write one additional example of each WHAT mindfulness skill.

In a group setting, choose an object to practice the WHAT skills. Practitioners can also choose a mindfulness activity listed in the pages of this activity book. After noticing the object for 1-2 minutes, ask each child to describe it.

Suggestions for the Therapists

Ask the child and caregiver to review the homework assignment prior to leaving your office to ensure they understand the task.

Request the child (with caregiver's help) to memorize the WHAT skills and a description of each.

WHAT Mindfulness Skills

Write one example of each WHAT mindfulness skill during the week.

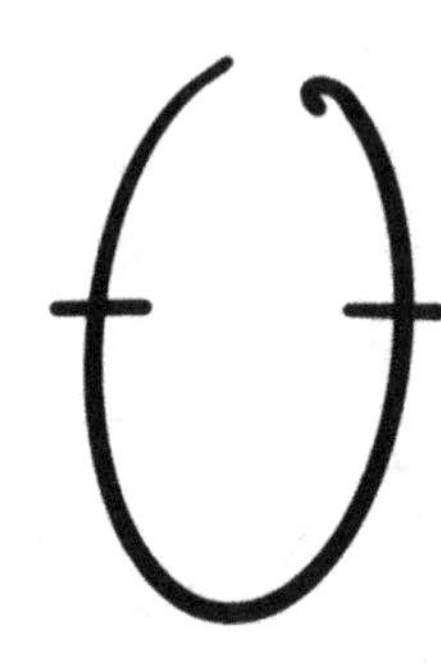

OBSERVE

- "I notice the feeling of tension in my shoulders."
- "I observe the feather is light and fluffy."
-

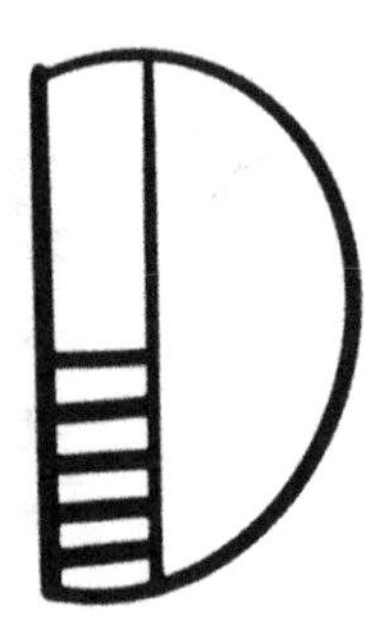

DESCRIBE

- "I feel scared and my throat is tight."
- "My baby sister is crying; she has tears on her cheeks."
-

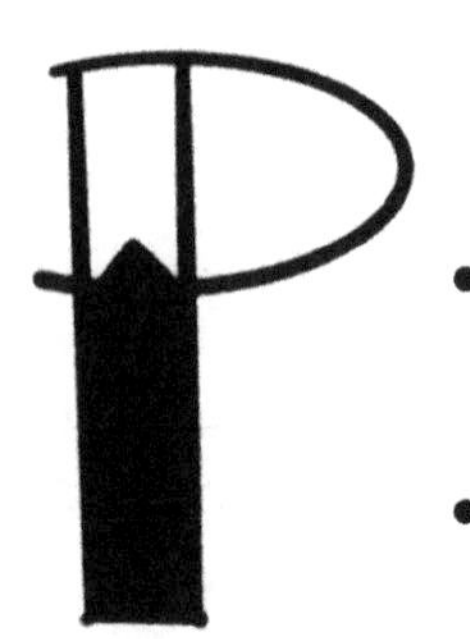

PARTICIPATE

- "I'm riding my bike, feeling the wind on my face with no worries of who may be watching me."
-

Adapted from Linehan, *DBT Skills Training Manual* (2015b)

3. HOW SKILLS

The HOW skills consist of nonjudgmentally, one-mindfully, and effectively. These skills are done all at the same time, and teach kids *how* to practice their mindfulness. For example, they observe in a nonjudgmental, one-mindful, and effective way.

"Being nonjudgmental is sticking to the facts, and noticing only what you observe with your senses."

- Nonjudgmentally is noticing without judging or evaluating. Instead, stick to the facts: who, what, when, where, and how. Stay away from evaluating things as "good" or "bad," "should" or "shouldn't."
- One-mindfully is doing one thing at a time in the present moment. It is the opposite of multi-tasking. For example, when a child is reading, they read with all of their attention and awareness to the experience. They resist the urge to read and also watch TV, and color.
- Effectively is doing what needs to be done, using skills to meet your goals. It is letting go of seeking revenge, and thoughts of "right" or "wrong," and "fair" or "unfair."

Handout Directions

Discuss the three HOW skills and provide examples of each. Just like the WHAT skills, incorporate all learning styles as you teach the HOW skills; explain the skills, point out the letters as visual images to aid in recalling the skills, and practice the HOW skills in session.

Discussion Questions

- Typically, who do you judge more —yourself or others?
- In daily life, do you notice judgmental thoughts? (Reminder: To change a thought from judgmental to nonjudgmental, describe it with facts.)
- Is it hard for you to let go of evaluating people, their behavior, and events as good or bad?
- What are your goals to be effective with family, friends, and school?
- Share an example of a time you were effective.

Mindfulness Skills

NONJUDGMENTALLY

Pay attention without deciding if situations are good or bad. Stick to what you can see and name the facts: who, what, where, how, and why.

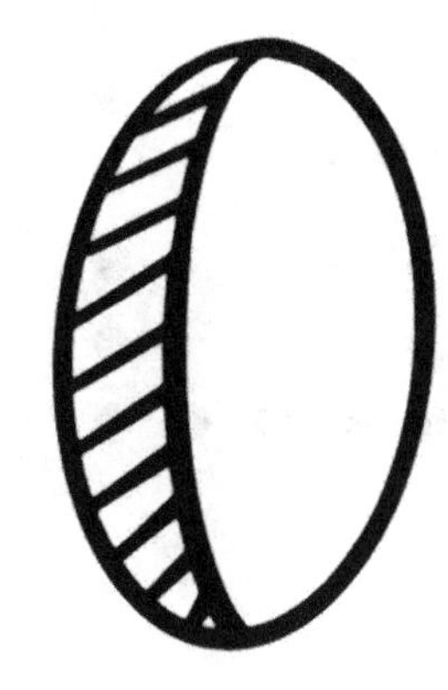

ONE-MINDFULLY

Do one thing at a time, in the current moment. Being one-mindful is opposite to multi-tasking. If you get distracted while being mindful, bring your attention back to the moment.

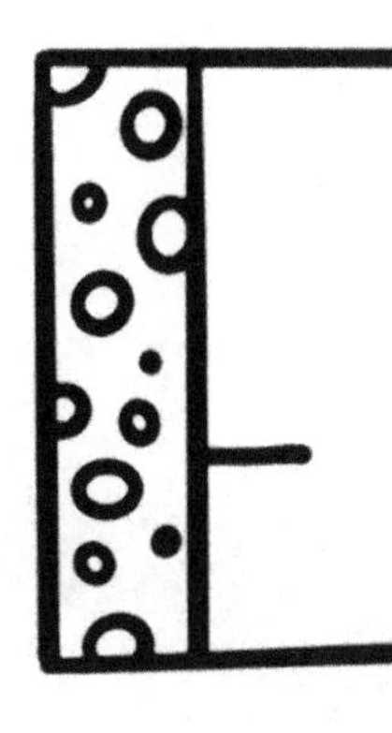

EFFECTIVELY

Being effective is playing by the rules. It's doing what works in the moment, without allowing emotions to get you off track. It is letting go of being "right" or seeking revenge.

Adapted from Linehan, *DBT Skills Training Manual* (2015b)

Worksheet Directions

On this worksheet there is one example provided under each skill. Write one additional example of each HOW mindfulness skill.

In a group setting, provide an object or an activity from this activity book. After the brief mindfulness practice, allow the children to describe their experience of being nonjudgmental, one-mindful, and effective.

Suggestions for the Therapists

Ask the child (with caregiver's help) to memorize the HOW skills and their descriptions. It is important for the child to know the skill in order to implement it into daily life.

Mindfulness Skills

Write one example of each HOW mindfulness skill during the week.

NONJUDGMENTALLY

- "Jodi turned away from me when I walked into class."
-

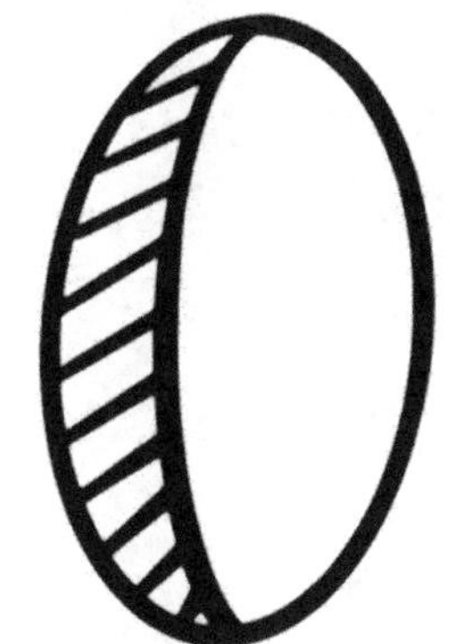

ONE-MINDFULLY

- "I put my phone down when mom wanted my full attention to talk."
-

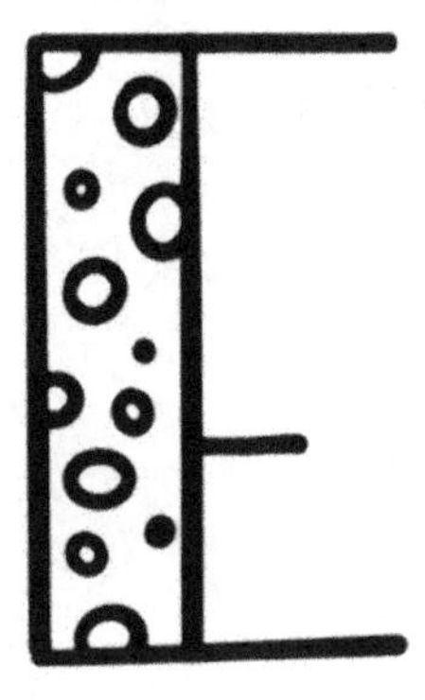

EFFECTIVELY

- "I'm going to talk to my dad even though I want to yell at him."
-

Adapted from Linehan, *DBT Skills Training Manual* (2015b)

4. ANCHORING

In a mindfulness practice, people often find it challenging to stay in the present moment. They can get sidetracked by past memories or future worries, or their thoughts may wander.

Anchoring is a place to return your focus when your mindfulness is interrupted. As soon as you notice being out of the moment, use an anchor to mindfully refocus your attention back to the present. There are several ways to anchor back to the present moment: the breath, the body, words, and counting. Let's look at each one.

The breath- Pay attention to your breath as you inhale through your nose, and exhale out of your mouth. Notice the "cool" feeling with the inhale, and the "warm" feeling of the exhale.

The body- Notice your stomach or chest as they move with your breath. The stomach or chest will rise as you breathe in, and fall as you breathe out. Practitioners can use the image of a balloon in the chid's belly which expands with an inhale causing their stomach to rise. In turn, the balloon will deflate as the child exhales the breathe, causing the stomach to fall. It may be easier for children to create this imagine if they lay on the floor, and see their stomach rise and fall.

Words- Use words such as peace, love, safe, kind, courage, brave, and calm to refocus your attention back to the moment. As you breathe in silently say a word yourself, and as you exhale say another.

Counting- There are multiple ways to anchor to the moment with counting. One way is to inhale and exhale, and count "one." As you inhale and exhale on the next breath, count "two." Continue to the count of five.

A second way is to inhale to the count of "one," and exhale to the count of "two." Continue counting this way four to five times.

Remind the kids that in order for the anchor to be successful, they need to mindfully shift their focus away from the distraction and to the anchor. In other words if they are counting and also thinking of the distraction, the anchor will not be as effective.

Note: There is only a handout for this skill.

Discussion Questions

- What distracts you the most when you practice mindfulness: distractions, wandering thoughts, memories of the past, or worries of the future?
- If you are using a word anchor, which words do you plan to use?
- Which anchor did you like the best? Which one was the hardest to do?

Suggestions for the Therapist

Practice all of the anchors together in session. The children and caregivers are more likely to use an anchor outside of session if they have used it in session and are familiar with it.

Anchoring

In mindfulness, you may get distracted, sidetracked by past memories or future worries, or your mind may wander. At this time, return your attention using an anchor-- a place to mindfully focus your attention and come back to the present moment. Which anchor will help you to refocus your attention?

The Breath- Pay attention to your breath. How does it feel as you breathe In through your nose, and exhale out of your mouth?

The Body- Notice your stomach or chest as it rises and falls with your breathing.

Words - Come back to the moment with words. As you breathe in, say a word like, "Peace," and as you exhale, say a different word -- "Love."

Counting- As you breathe in and out, count from 1 – 10. You can also breathe in for the count of 1, and out for the count of 2.

5. MINDFUL ACTIVITIES

Following are a few mindfulness activities to try in session with the child and caregiver, or group of children. The first two sheets are coloring pages for the children to mindfully color. These are followed by the activity, "Bubbles," to practice letting go of thoughts, emotions, or body sensations. Next is an activity sheet to teach the kids mindful breathing, and how to focus their attention.
Note: There are only handouts for these mindful activities.

a. Two Coloring Sheets

There are two coloring pages; the first one has larger spaces for younger children to color, and the second one has smaller spaces for older kids. The larger space is better suited for younger children who have less developed fine motor skills.

Handout Directions

As you color pay attention to yourself internally, and externally with your five senses. Pay attention with your sense of sound, sight, smell, and touch . . . there is not anything to taste! For example, notice the sound of the pencil or crayon on paper, the sight of the shapes on the page and the coloring marks, the smell of the pencils or paper, and the way the pencil feels in your hand.

Internally, notice any thoughts, feelings, or body sensations. For example, while you color the page, do you having judging thoughts about yourself or your coloring ability?

Discussion Questions

Following the coloring activity, ask the kids and caregivers to describe their experience.

- What did you notice with your five senses?
- What did you notice internally?
- Did you experience any distracting or wandering thoughts, or drifting from the present to the future or past?

Coloring Page

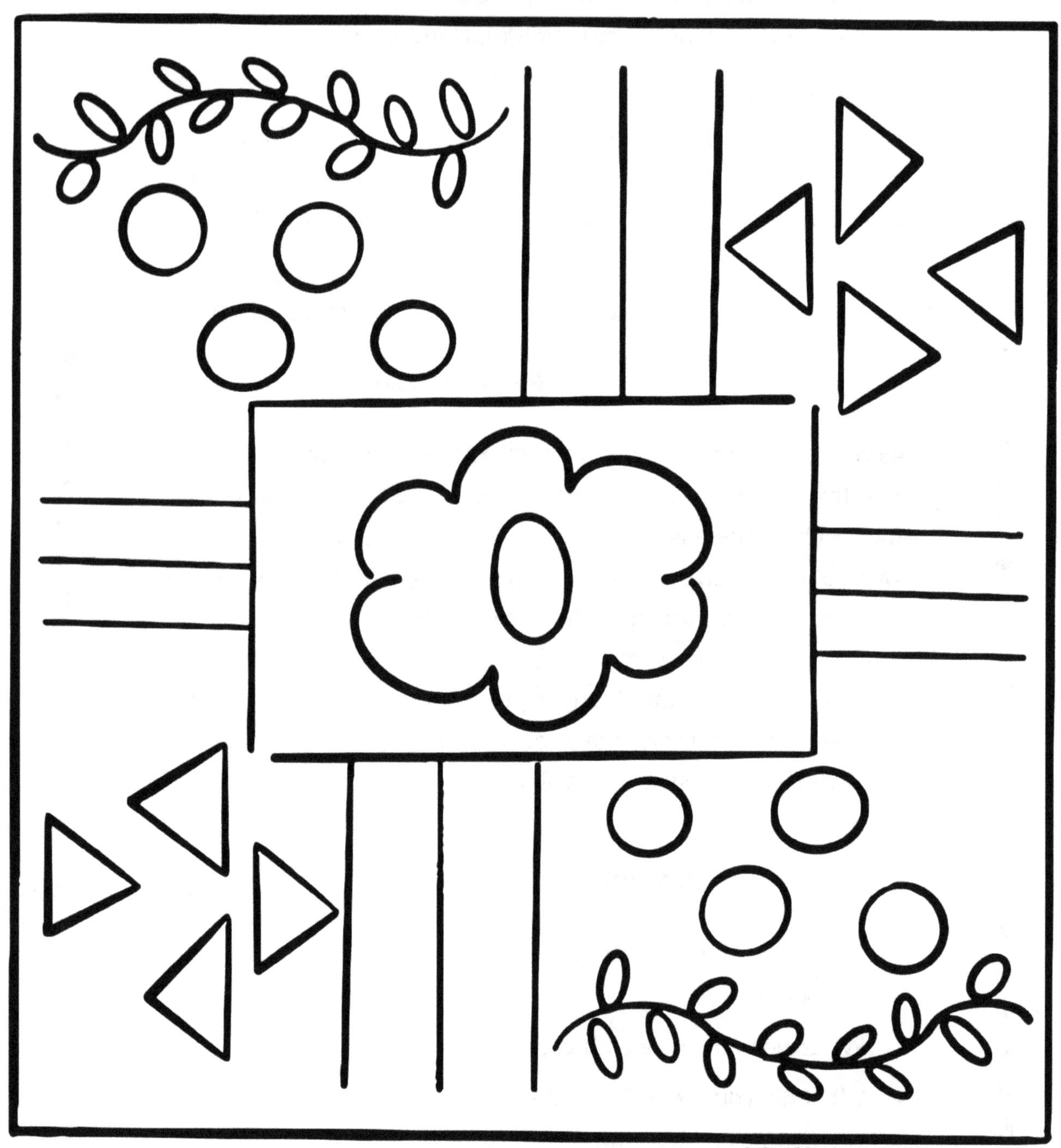

Coloring Page

b. Bubbles

Sometimes, kids encounter unwanted thoughts or emotions, and linger on them. If they persist, it can lead to dysregulation of emotion or behavior.

"Once the child is more aware of their environment, move the practice to awareness of self, the child's body and behavior."

The bubbles mindfulness activity teaches kids and caregivers the ability to notice a thought, feeling, memory, or body sensation and let it go. There are similar activities in adult and adolescent DBT with many variations, a couple often used examples are, "Watching Train Cars" and "Watching Clouds in the Sky."

Note: There is only a handout for this activity.

Handout Directions

Explain to the children that the mindfulness activity will teach them to let go of unwanted or negative thoughts, feelings, memory, or sensations.

Instruct the child to sit up in a comfortable and alert position. Tell them to look at their paper, "Notice any thoughts, feelings, memories, or sensations rise up in your mind; imagine them rising up in a bubble."

Continue to say to the child, "As each bubble rises silently ask yourself, "What is inside of it?" If it's a thought, pay attention to it, and watch it float away; mark that bubble with a "T." Is it a feeling? Notice it and watch it float away; mark that bubble with an "F." Memories in a bubble are marked with an "M," and mark "S" for any sensations."

If the child runs out of bubbles, instruct them to draw more on the page.

Discussion Questions

- What happens when you hang on to unwanted or negative thoughts, feelings, or memories?
- Have you experienced a time when you continued to think about unwanted or negative thoughts, feelings, or memories? If yes, how did it turn out?
- Does it turn out differently when you let them go?

Suggestions for the Therapist

Make sure the child understands they are only to write an initial in the bubble and not an explanation of a situation, thought, or memory. In one of my groups, a teen misunderstood the instructions and wrote out detailed information about a distressing situation. Needless to say, the teen felt more distraught after the mindfulness activity than before it started.

Mindfulness Skills

RISING BUBBLES

Mindfulness helps kids to feel calm and focused. One mindfulness practice is rising bubbles; it's letting thoughts and feelings go instead of holding on to them.

Imagine bubbles slowly rising up in front of you. As the bubbles rise, imagine that each one contains a thought, feeling, or body sensation. Notice what's inside the bubble . . . is a thought? feeling? sensation? Mark the bubbles accordingly with a T, F, or S. After you notice it, let it slowly float away; observe the next bubble as it rises.

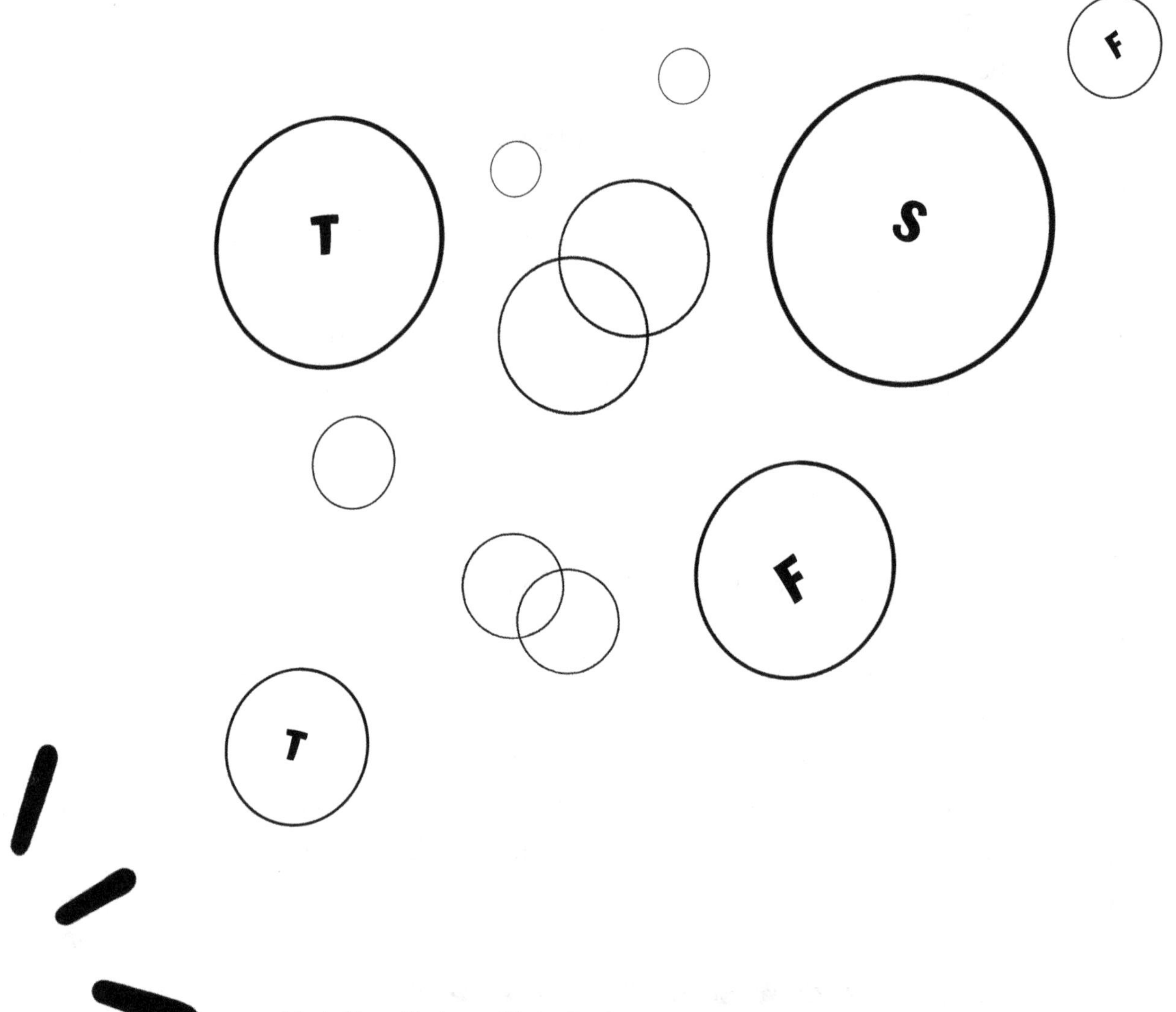

Adapted from Hooker and Fodor, *Teaching Mindfulness to Children* (2008)

c. Sniff the Flower, Blow Out the Candle

This mindfulness exercise is an easy way to teach mindful breathing to young kids. Generally, breathing during mindfulness follows the child's natural rhythm; the breath should not be pushed out or held in. At the same time, mindfulness is most effective when a child inhales in their nose, and then exhales out of their mouth.

"Be creative with this mindfulness activity! For example, you can change it to 'Smell the s'mores and cool it off with your breath.'"

This is also a good first mindfulness exercise because the image naturally makes sense to children. When the child sees the image of a flower they know to sniff or breathe in. Likewise, the child already understands to breathe out in order to blow out birthday candles.

Note: There is only a handout for this activity.

Handout Directions

The main purpose of this handout is to teach children a simple mindfulness activity. The handout's images quickly convey the process of mindful breathing. Invite the child to look at the illustration of the flower; ask them to breathe in their nose and pretend they are sniffing the flower. Next, instruct them to breathe out of their mouth, pretending they are gently blowing out birthday candles. Tell them to sniff the flower and blow out the candle four times.

Discussion Questions

- Which type of flower do you like best? Rose, tulip, carnation?
- What color is your flower?
- When would be a good time to use this breathing activity?

Suggestions for the Therapist

Allow the children time to color their flower and candle.

Remind the children not to hold their breath, or blow it out too quickly. This may be tempting for some kids as they like to forcefully blow out the birthday candles! Ask them to take their time and breathe naturally.

This activity can also be done with a pretend pizza. Ask the children to hold out their hand as though they are holding a plate with a hot slice of pizza. Instruct them to smell the pizza as they inhale, and blow on it (exhale) to cool it off. There are many other similar activities . . . be creative and have fun!

Mindfulness Skills

Sniff the flower,
Blow out the candle

Taking deep breaths helps you to feel calm and peaceful. One fun way to practice your breathing is-- sniff the flower, blow out the candle.

Looking at the picture below, imagine sniffing the flower (breathe in through your nose), and then blowing out the candle (blow the breath out of your mouth . . . just like blowing out birthday candles). Repeat this pattern of breathing four times.

sniff the flower

blow out the candle

SECTION 3

Distress Tolerance

Distress tolerance skills teach children to tolerate and survive emotional crises without making the situation worse with impulsive behavior. In fact, DBT points out that there are advantages to tolerating pain in a skillful way as pain is a part of life and can not be avoided.

Distress tolerance skills are divided into two groups: crisis survival and reality acceptance.

"DBT points out that there are advantages to tolerating pain in a skillful way as pain is a part of life and can not be avoided."

Crisis survival skills help the child to problem solve, and to manage a painful situation without making it worse. The reality acceptance skills give children the ability to accept a situation as it is without trying to change it, avoid it, or fight against it.

In the activity book we cover the distress tolerance skills in DBT-C including: Letting It Go, STOP skills, DISTRACT, Willfulness and Willingness, Pros and Cons, and Self-Soothing. In addition, the book covers Which Road?, TIP skills, and Items in My Self-Soothe Box.

1. WHICH ROAD WILL YOU CHOOSE?

Which road will you choose? is a new distress tolerance skill adapted from the adult and adolescent DBT skill, turning the mind. Typically, this is the first skill to teach from the distress tolerance module. Practitioners can incorporate this skill into their practice as much or as little as they choose since it is not a traditional skill. In my practice, I use the skill to build the child's self-awareness through observing which road they are on, and which road is most effective for them. Children are often faced with two decisions: to accept reality as it is or reject it. This skill helps them to accept realities that feel unacceptable.

The illustration on the handout shows two roads; the road to the left is "rejecting" and the road to the right is "agreeing." When kids are on the rejecting road they are rejecting reality; a few examples on this road are refusing to follow rules, accept consequences, share feelings, or listen. This gives kids pain, unwanted emotions, and a life they do not want. The behaviors on this road may not always occur deliberately nevertheless they still lead to misery. Thus the outcome on this road is depicted by a broken heart indicating a life of suffering.

On the other hand, when a child is on the agreeing road it demonstrates they are willing to accept reality. Some behaviors on this road include: obeying rules, accepting consequences, sharing feelings, and listening. Living life on the agreeing road is effective, and will lead to better outcomes. The symbol for the agreeing road and its outcome is a smiling sunshine.

On the sheet, there is an illustration of a pathway from the rejecting road to the agreeing road. The pathway is an opportunity for the child to notice their internal "clues" (feelings, thoughts, sensations, urges) that indicate they are on the rejecting road. Then, they can make a wise decision to behave skillfully and get back on the agreeing road. Of course, this road ends with better outcomes and a sunny face. The pathway remains available to the children at all times as they can always make a wise choice.

Handout Directions

Explain the skill to the child and caregiver, or group of children.

1. **Notice you are on the rejecting road.** Pay attention to internal clues that indicate you are on the rejecting road; the clues include your feelings, thoughts, body sensations, and urges or actions. For example, feeling angry, thinking "I'm not going to do it!" with tense fists and an urge to throw things. Another example is feeling sad, refusing to talk, an urge to run away, and thinking, "No one cares about me."
2. **Think of a DBT skill to replace your ineffective or harmful behavior.** What skills can you use to replace your behavior with a skillful one? Some skills to try are: opposite action, half smiling and willing hands, or TIP skills. What skill might make the situation better?
3. **Do the skill!** Do the skill in a mindful way. Take your time and make a calm decision; stay in control and remain nonjudgmental.
4. **Cope ahead for future times you may be on the rejecting road.** Plan ahead for future times you are on the rejecting road so that you can choose to behave skillfully. Typically, what are the clues and recurring situations when you find yourself on the rejecting road? Write out a plan and include the skills you will use in the situations; you can also imagine or role play behaving skillfully.

Discussion Questions

- What are some of your clues on the rejecting road?
- How can you use the pathway to get back on the agreeing road?
- What are some of your usual clues on the agreeing road?
- Write out a cope ahead plan with one typical situation on the rejecting road.

Questions For Caregivers to Ask Their Child in Daily Life:

- Which road are you on right now? Accepting or Rejecting?
- What skill can you use to take the pathway over to the agreeing road?

Which Road will You Choose?

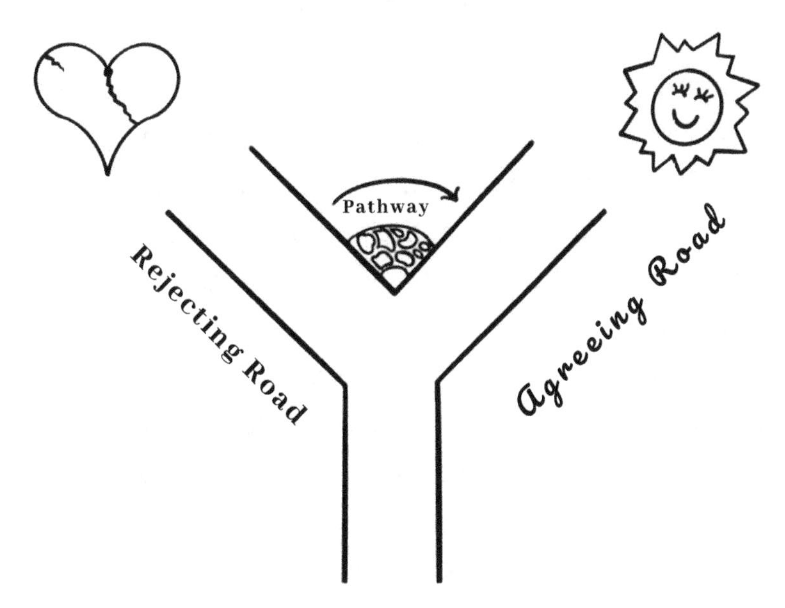

Children are often faced with two choices: to accept reality as it is ("agreeing" road) or reject it ("rejecting" road).

Some behaviors a child may show on the rejecting road are refusing to follow rules, share feelings, or listen. When kids stay on this road it gives them a life they don't want as shown by the broken heart.

On the other hand, kids can live life on the agreeing road. Behaviors on this road include: obeying rules, sharing feelings, and listening. The agreeing road leads to better outcomes as shown by a smiling sunshine.

When kids notice they are on the rejecting road, they can make a wise decision to take the stone pathway, and get back on the agreeing road.

Let's look at the steps to living life on the agreeing road:

1. Notice you're on the rejecting road by paying attention to your "clues:"
   - Thought
   - Feeling
   - Urge or Action
   - Body sensation
2. Think of a DBT skill to replace your ineffective or harmful behavior.
3. Do the DBT skill!
4. Cope ahead for future times you may be on the rejecting road.

Adapted from Linehan, *DBT Skills Training Manual* (2015b)

Worksheet Directions

The worksheet is introduced in session with the therapist. Choose a situation or ask the caregiver to identify a mild situation that commonly occurs at home. Encourage the child to discuss the situation, and notice the "clues" they experienced at the time. As the child describes each clue write it next to the title of thought, feeling, urge or action, and body sensation.

Brainstorm DBT skills that the child c an use to replace the ineffective behavior. Offer suggestions alongside the child or caregiver. Remember to positively reinforce them as they participate and name skills.

Encourage the child to choose a skill and, if possible, role play behaving skillfully.

Cope ahead for upcoming or repetitive situations, and write out a plan for them to implement.

Suggestions For The Therapist

It is critical that the child and caregiver do not get the impression that the rejecting road indicates "wrong" or "bad," or that the accepting road is "good" or "right" as this implies judgment. Anytime they use judging language, stop them and ask them to notice and describe, or use factual language instead.

This skill is introduced over several sessions. In the first session, explain the skill and discuss a few examples with the child and caregiver. Second, use a few examples and role play using the which road? skill. Third, ask the caregiver to role play with the child in session so that you may shape and reinforce behaviors.

When you notice the child is demonstrating rejecting road behaviors in session, increase the child's self awareness by prompting them to reflect which road they are on and what skills they could use to get back on the agreeing road. This is an important time to model the skill for caregivers too.

Which Road will You Choose?

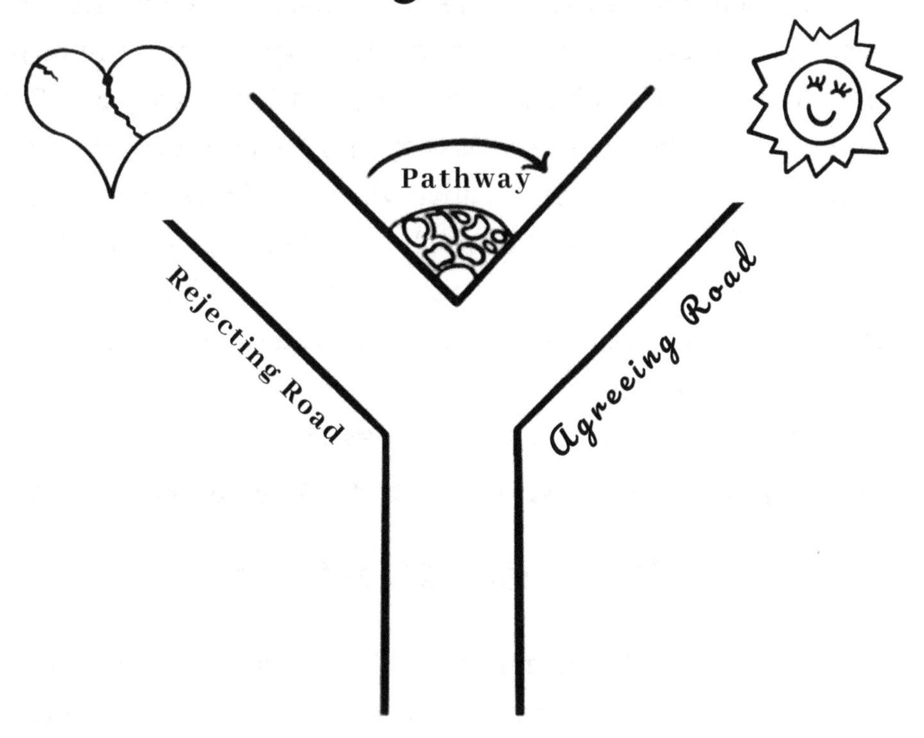

Situation:

1. **Notice I'm on the rejecting road; my clues are:**
   Thought:

   Feeling:

   Urge or Action:

   Body sensation:

2. **Think of a DBT skill to replace my ineffective or harmful behavior:**

3. **Do the DBT skill!**

4. **Cope ahead for future times I may be on the rejecting road.**

Adapted from Linehan, *DBT Skills Training Manual* (2015b)

2. HALF SMILE & WILLING HANDS

Half smile and willing hands are skills to help kids get through a difficult moment; they are the body's expression of reality acceptance. A child's body and facial expression effect their emotions. In turn, the child's emotions influence their body and facial expression. For example, when kids are nervous they may tap their foot, or when angry will throw objects. In addition, when a child is sitting upright and relaxed they are more likely to be alert. Whereas a child sitting slumped over is likely to feel depressed. When a child's body and facial expression show acceptance through half smile and willing hands, their emotions tend to follow.

Note: There is only a worksheet for this skill.

Worksheet Directions

Use the worksheet to explain half smile and willing hands. Before you begin the practice, describe how to tighten and relax the muscles in the body—including the face. It is easiest to start with tensing the hands into a fist, and then opening the hands with relaxation. Once they know how to tense and relax muscles, encourage them to do the skill alongside you and the caregiver. Explain to the children that being mindful is the foundation for both of these skills.

Discussion Questions

- Is half smiling phony?
- What are the pros and cons of using half smile and willing hands?
- What does it mean to be mindful while using this skill?

Suggestions for The Therapist

Practice several different smiles in front of a mirror so the kids can see their own facial expressions. Ask the children to notice and describe their internal and external experience with each smile.

Half Smile & Willing Hands

Our emotions and body are often connected i.e., when kids are nervous, they might tap their foot. Half smiling and willing hands help kids get through a challenging moment and accept the situation. When a kid's body and facial expression show acceptance, his or her emotions will follow.
Let's look at how to practice both half smile and willing hands:

HALF SMILE

Try to make a relaxed, agreeing face. Relax the muscles in your face, and make a small smile. Mindfully notice your half smile. If you want, gently hold a pencil in your mouth. If your smile is too big, the pencil will fall out.
Lastly, remember not to let your smile go into a phony grin. Phony looks sarcastic to others and stirs unwanted emotions in you.

WILLING HANDS

Open your hands and put them on your lap or by your sides. Place your hands palms up and relax your fingers. Mindfully notice your willing hands.

PRACTICE

Just like any other habit, practice makes it easier to do in stressful moments. First, try it right now! Secondly, practice over the week and keep track of your practice below.

MON	TUES	WED	THURS	FRI	SAT	SUN

3. LETTING IT GO

Letting it go is a DBT-C skill adapted from the adult DBT skill, radical acceptance. The skill helps kids to face realities or truths in life they cannot change or control, a few examples include: a friend moving away, losing a pet, or a change in the family. It helps if they can "let go" of trying to control or change a situation, and learn to accept it instead.

Acceptance is not approval or giving up. It is acknowledging the reality even when you do not like it. When a child is accepting, they accept the situation fully with their mind, heart, and body.

Handout Directions

Discuss the steps of letting it go. The first step is to notice their internal "clues" of not accepting a truth or reality. Next, they take four breaths and silently saying an acceptance statement. Lastly, the children will match their behavior to acceptance with half smile, willing hands, or opposite action.

Discussion Questions

- The greatest acceptance is the statement—all things are perfect just as they are. What do you think about this?
- What are some things that have been hard for you to let go of in the past?
- When you accept, that does not mean you have to agree with it. Does this idea make it easier to accept?

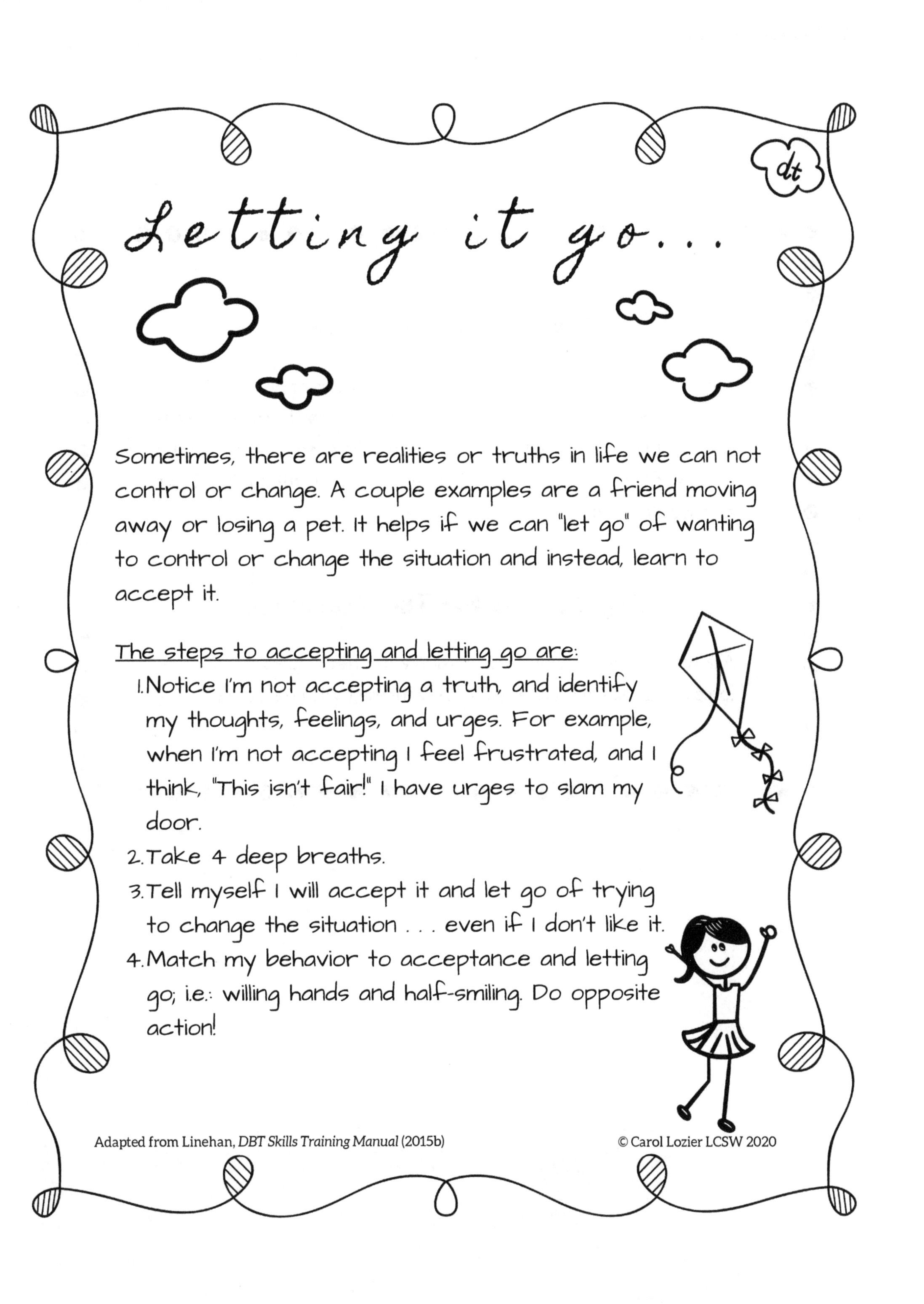

Letting it go...

Sometimes, there are realities or truths in life we can not control or change. A couple examples are a friend moving away or losing a pet. It helps if we can "let go" of wanting to control or change the situation and instead, learn to accept it.

<u>The steps to accepting and letting go are:</u>

1. Notice I'm not accepting a truth, and identify my thoughts, feelings, and urges. For example, when I'm not accepting I feel frustrated, and I think, "This isn't fair!" I have urges to slam my door.
2. Take 4 deep breaths.
3. Tell myself I will accept it and let go of trying to change the situation . . . even if I don't like it.
4. Match my behavior to acceptance and letting go; i.e.: willing hands and half-smiling. Do opposite action!

Adapted from Linehan, *DBT Skills Training Manual* (2015b)

Worksheet Directions

This worksheet can be done in session for practice or given as homework. When the skill is practiced in session, role play the steps. Encourage the child to identify their clues aloud, take deep breaths, say the acceptance statement aloud; and show half smile, willing hands, or an opposite action.

Suggestions for The Therapist

Ask the caregiver to practice in session with the child. Positively reinforce the caregiver's behavior as they interact with the child.

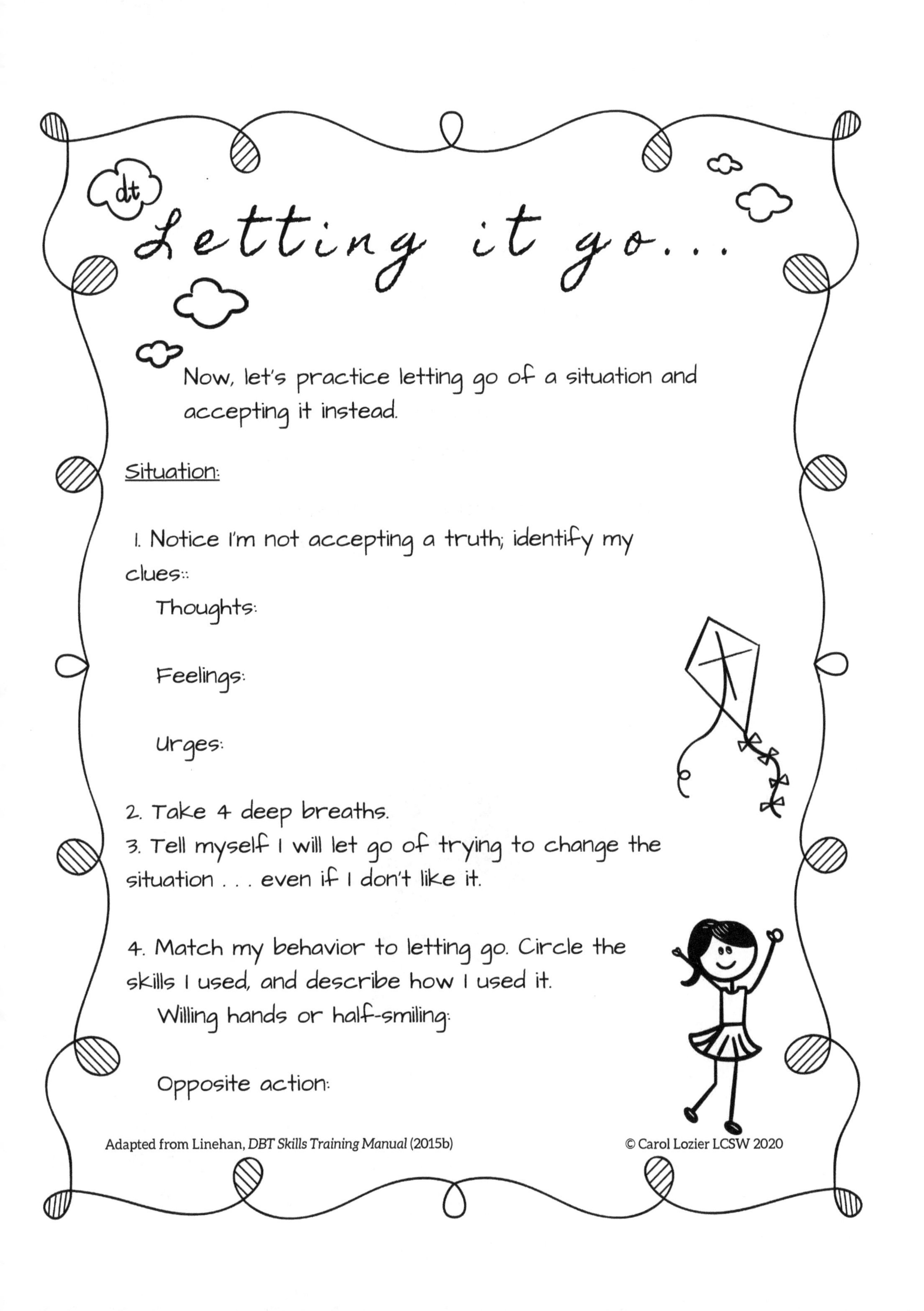

Letting it go...

Now, let's practice letting go of a situation and accepting it instead.

Situation:

1. Notice I'm not accepting a truth; identify my clues::

    Thoughts:

    Feelings:

    Urges:

2. Take 4 deep breaths.
3. Tell myself I will let go of trying to change the situation . . . even if I don't like it.

4. Match my behavior to letting go. Circle the skills I used, and describe how I used it.

    Willing hands or half-smiling:

    Opposite action:

Adapted from Linehan, *DBT Skills Training Manual* (2015b)

4. STOP SKILLS

The STOP skills are a distress tolerance skill to help kids be less impulsive in their actions and decision making. STOP skills were first introduced to me in 1990 at my job at a residential treatment center for children in San Diego, California. At the treatment center STOP was explained to the children using concrete concepts which is how it will be described to the reader.

"The STOP skills are a distress tolerance skill to help kids be less impulsive in their actions and decision making."

As children develop a better understanding of the skill, they are more likely to use it and behave skillfully during times of high stress.

Handout Directions

Explain the goal of the STOP skills, and describe each step to the child and caregiver or to the group of children. STOP is an acronym and each of the letters indicate a step in the process.

In the first step, S indicates stop and freeze; ask the child to show their freeze pose. Most kids immediately understand this request from playing the game, freeze tag. Practitioners can also mention the which road? skill. Discuss paying attention to their clues that signify they are in emotion mind and on the rejecting road, these are both clear signs to use the STOP skills.

The next step is T which signifies take a deep breath and think. This step helps them to pause for a moment, and initiate their thinking process which begins to balance their high emotion. Once they are more regulated, they can think clearly.

Now, use wise mind to determine three options or ways to solve the problem, and identify the outcome of each solution. In this step, O stands for both options and outcomes. Allow the kids to name positive and negative choices. In the beginning, they will tend to only name positive ones, but we want them to consider all choices which reflects true-life decision making.

Lastly, the children choose one solution that has a positive outcome. In this step, the P signifies pick the best one and proceed with this choice mindfully.

Discussion Questions

- What are some impulsive urges or behaviors that let you know to STOP? (You can also ask, What are some rejecting road clues that let you know to STOP?)
- Why do we think of all possible solutions, ones with positive and negative outcomes?
- Once you have chosen a solution, describe how you will do it mindfully.

STOP

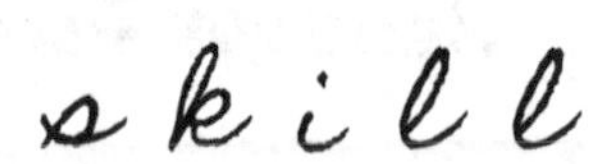

The STOP skill helps kids to be less impulsive (i.e., fight or run away) because impulsive behaviors only make situations worse. Let's look at each letter of the STOP skill:

1.Stop.
When you begin to feel like your emotions are going to take over, stop and freeze in place. Don't react to your feelings or the situation.

2. Take a deep breath & Think.
Taking a deep breath calms your body which helps you to be more self-aware and think clearly. It also gives you the chance to think of other ways to handle the situation instead of reacting.

3. Options and Outcomes.
Now that you are more self-aware and in control, use wise mind to think of three ways to solve the situation. Also, figure out the outcome for each solution (will it turn out well or cause more problems?).

4. Pick the most effective one and proceed (go!)
Consider your choices and their outcome. Does the choice make the situation better or worse? Ask your wise mind how to deal with the problem. Choose a solution that will lead to a positive outcome, and do it mindfully.

Adapted from Linehan, *DBT Skills Training Manual* (2015b)

Worksheet Directions

This worksheet is used in session and assigned as homework. Since you have already explained the skill to kids and caregivers, role play several situations. First, make up a few situations to practice, and then ask the child or caregiver to provide true-life examples. Once the child has role played several of these situations, encourage the caregiver and child to role play with practitioner as the observer to offer feedback and encouragement. As you role play, stand up and act out the situations; role plays are an active practice!

Suggestions for The Therapist

When children are first learning STOP skills, and if the caregiver agrees, write the word "STOP" on the back of their hand. This prompts the child to use the skill. In order to avoid habituation, advise the caregiver to use different colors and placements of the word "STOP" on each of the child's hands.

Continue to define new DBT language as you describe this skill. At this point, the child and caregiver have learned some DBT words therefore ask them to define familiar words as you encounter them.

STOP

skill

Situation:

1. Stop and freeze in place

2. Take a deep breath & Think

3. Options (choices) & Outcomes (how does it turn out?)

Options (choices)	Outcomes (how does it turn out?)
1.	1.
2.	2.
3.	3.

4. Pick the most effective one & "proceed" . . . go!

Write it here . . .

Adapted from Linehan, *DBT Skills Training Manual* (2015b)

5. TIP SKILLS

TIP is an acronym that stands for temperature, intense exercise, and paced breathing. TIP skills are used when a child is in a fight, flight, or freeze response, times when it is difficult for them to manage extreme emotions or to think clearly. TIP skills are easy to use and work quickly to lower the child's arousal; then, they can follow it with additional skills. The TIP skills reduce physical arousal by stimulating the parasympathetic nervous system (PNS); this system helps the body to calm. Let's look at each letter of the TIP skills.

Tip the temperature of the body. Cooling off the face helps to decrease the child's emotions. If they are unwilling to cool off their face, ask them to apply cold to the body. A few ways to tip the body temperature are: hold an ice pack or splash cold water on the face, hold a piece of ice, drink ice water, step outside if it is cold, and eat a popsicle.

Intense exercise. Intense aerobic exercise allows kids to have a physical action (hit, run, throw) for their emotion (anger, fear). Twenty minutes of intense exercise helps to reduce a child's negative mood and to increase their positive emotions. Encourage the child to find fun ways to exercise, such as: jump rope, hula hoop, skip it, basketball, hop scotch, baseball, running, tennis, volleyball, hiking, walking, playing on the playground, kick the can, and tag. There are so many fun ways to exercise; let the kids know—if their heart is pumping, they are doing intense exercise.

Paced breathing. Unlike the other two TIP skills, paced breathing can be used in any setting to help the child relax and calm. Introduce various ways to practice paced breathing, and practice them together in session.

The easiest paced breathing for kids to learn is "Sniff the Flower, Blow the Candle" (this handout is located in the mindfulness module). Another easy one is square breathing; an illustration of it is shown on the handout. In square breathing, the child traces (or gazes) the arrows with their finger beginning at the top left corner as they take an inhale in the nose. As they progress onto the next side of the square they pause with the breath; then, they trace across to the left on the bottom side and exhale out of their mouth. On the final side, they trace up and pause the breath again. Once the reach the top left corner, they begin again. The child traces around the square four to five times.

Handout Directions

Discuss each of the TIP skills with the child and caregiver. Practitioners will explain each skill and name examples within each skill.

Ask the child to identify an example of a situation that causes mild emotional dysregulation. Along side the child, role play the situation, and prompt the child to use each of the TIP skills. Have ice available for the child to use in session.

Discussion Questions

- When you have strong emotions and can not think clearly what urges or behaviors do you experience? (This question can be answered by both child and caregiver.)
- Have you ever held ice or splashed cold water on your face? If not, would you be willing to try it the next time you have strong emotions?
- What are some fun aerobic exercises you like to do?
- What is one intense exercise you would be willing to try next time you are in emotion mind?
- Would you be willing for your caregiver to remind you to use TIP skills? If yes, what word, phrase, or sign would you like your caregiver to use?

TIP *Skills*

TIP YOUR BODY TEMPERATURE

Tip the temperature of your face to cool off your emotions. Put something cold on your face to calm your emotions. If you're unwilling to cool off your face, hold something cold to your body. For example, hold an ice pack on your forehead or cheeks, splash cold water on your face, or drink ice water.

INTENSE EXERCISE

Intense exercise gets your heart rate up, and your emotions calming down. A few examples are jumping jacks, four square, hop scotch, hula hoop, dancing, and jumping rope. Do fun exercises that get your heart pumping!

PACED BREATHING

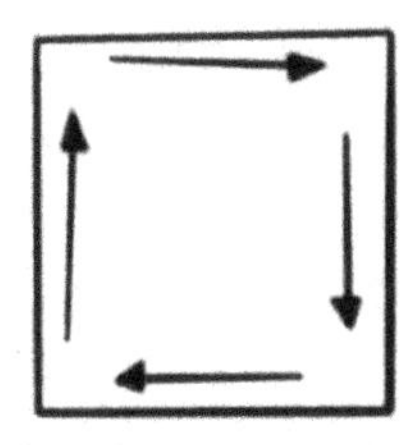

Paced breathing helps your body to relax. As your breathe out calming breaths, your emotions will calm too. There are many ways to practice paced breathing; the easiest is to breathe and count. Breathe in your nose and count "one," and count "one" as your exhale out of your mouth. Then, count "two" as you inhale, and "two" as you exhale; keep going to the count of five.

Adapted from Linehan, *DBT Skills Training Manual* (2015b)

Worksheet Directions

This sheet can be given to the child and caregiver for homework. In session, after you have discussed the TIP skills, write examples of individual skills the child is willing to try. Over the week she will try them, and then note the ones she found to be helpful. Before the child and caregiver leave the session, ask them to repeat the word, phrase, or sign they agreed upon as a signal to use TIP skills during times of distress.

Suggestions to The Therapist

Practice this skill in session, actively do all three skills alongside the child. As previously stated, the child is more likely to use the skills in her own environment if she already practiced them in session.

If the child becomes dysregulated during any session, prompt them to use this skill. Stop and get some ice, and hand it to the child in a cup or paper towel. Encourage the child to do an exercise (jumping jacks or burpees) and paced breathing with you.

TIP *Skills*

What TIP skills are you willing to try? What TIP skills have you found to be most helpful?

TIP YOUR BODY TEMPERATURE

Willing to try:

Helpful:

INTENSE EXERCISE

Willing to try:

Helpful:

PACED BREATHING

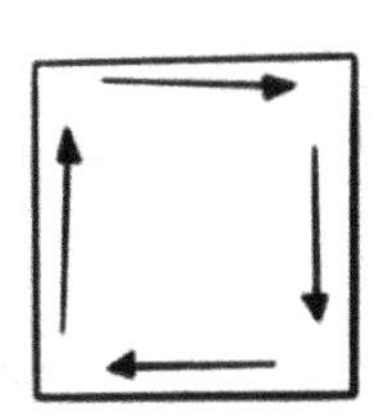

Willing to try:

Helpful:

Adapted from Linehan, DBT Skills Training Manual (2015b)

6. DISTRACT

The DISTRACT skills enable children to find distance from their urge by doing something else while waiting for the urge to lessen. The DISTRACT skills are meant to help kids tolerate their urge, and get through a situation without making it worse. Also, some of the DISTRACT skills replace a negative event for a more positive one. The DISTRACT skill is a combination of the adult and teen DBT skills of wise mind ACCEPTS and IMPROVE the moment. Let's learn each letter of the skill, DISTRACT.

Do Something Else Change your focus by doing something that really captures your attention. A few examples are: read your favorite book series, play a card game, watch your favorite cartoon or show, play tag with the neighborhood kids, make your favorite dessert, and jump on a trampoline.

Imagine Being Somewhere Else Imagine being somewhere that brings up relaxing or safe feelings for you. Imagine being in your favorite spot in your home, at the beach or in the woods, or at the home of a close relative like grandparents or cousins.

Use Your Five Senses to Distract Your Focus Away From Pain Draw attention away from your pain with your five senses. Look at pictures of cute animals or your own pet, smell your favorite essential oil or candle, chew tasty gum or ice, crawl under a cozy blanket, hold your stuffed animal, listen to your favorite or uplifting music.

Take a Short Vacation Take a short break or vacation, from 10 minutes to 2 hours, in order to decompress and regroup. This is a planned activity (kids need to ask permission) and not an abrupt exit to avoid or run away from a situation. Take a short nap, go to a friend or relatives home, make a fort and hang out in it, play in your tree house.

Read Read to distract yourself and create positive emotions. Read all kinds of books-fiction, nonfiction, historical fiction, comic books, biographies, kid's magazines, and activity books.

Do Arts and Crafts Do arts and crafts activities to distract your attention.

Paint, draw, color, crochet, knit, make friendship bracelets, make slime, use play dough or clay, build with craft sticks and many others.

Contribute and Do Something Nice for Someone When you contribute by doing nice things for others, it takes the focus off of yourself and your own pain. In addition, once you have completed the task, it creates positive emotions for you. Mow your neighbor's yard, shovel the neighbor's driveway, help your teacher clean the classroom or help clean your own home, volunteer to watch a younger sibling while mom makes dinner, let your siblings watch tv even though it is your turn.

Keep Your Thoughts Busy Distract your attention by keeping your thoughts busy. Count dots on the ceiling, do your multiplication tables, do a sudoku puzzle, and do the categories game using various categories. In the categories game, name items that begin with letter A all the way through Z, that fit into the named category. For example, our category is animals: antelope, bison, cougar, donkey, and so on through letter Z.

Handout Directions

The DISTRACT skill is another acronym; each letter stands for a different activity that helps the child tolerate their urge. The purpose of the DISTRACT skills are for the child to create distance from the urge by doing an activity, and while they are occupied, it allows their urge to decrease. Explain each of the letters and their skill, and name a few activities that fall under each skill.

Discussion Questions

- How can you maintain a balance of creating space from the urge, and still not fall into avoiding or isolating behaviors?
- What DISTRACT skills have you already tried, and found them to be helpful and effective?

DISTRACT

Tolerate painful feelings and urges so you don't make things worse.

D *Do something else that grabs your attention.*
Examples: watch your favorite cartoon or a very funny show, do an interesting science experiment, make a dessert, go outside and study nature, jump on a trampoline.

I *Imagine being somewhere else.*
Examples: Imagine a relaxing or safe place (at the beach or in the woods, your favorite spot in your home or at the home of a close relative).

5 senses

S *Use your 5 senses to distract you away from your pain.*
Examples: hold ice, take a warm bath or shower, smell your favorite essential oil, crawl under a cozy blanket, listen to relaxing music, look at a picture of someone (or an animal) you adore, hold your stuffed animal.

T *Take a short vacation.*
Examples: Swing on a swing set, play outside in your tree house, play at a friend's house, make a fort and hang out in it.

R *Read all types of books!*
Examples: Read fiction, nonfiction, historical fiction, kid's magazines, activity books, comic books, biographies, and even Mad Libs.

A *Do arts and crafts projects.*
Examples: make slime, draw, paint, make a collage, crochet, sew, practice origami, make friendship bracelets, play dough or clay, do a puzzle and then glue it.

C *Contribute and do something nice for someone.*
Examples: shovel snow off your neighbor's driveway, clean the kitchen at home, help your teacher clean the classroom, let your siblings watch a show even though it's your turn.

T *Keep your thoughts busy.*
Examples: do Sudoku puzzles, count objects in a room, do multiplication tables, do the categories game from A to Z using various categories.

Adapted from Linehan, *DBT Skills Training Manual* (2015b)

Worksheet Directions

In session with the child and caregiver or in a group, have a whiteboard available to list activity ideas. Under each letter of the DISTRACT skills, name the skill and describe it, and then brainstorm a list of activities that fall under each skill.

Suggestions For The Therapist

Therapists, be aware of negative peer pressure in the group setting. Children may lose interest in trying activities when they hear peers making negative comments about them. Encourage the kids to be open and willing to try numerous activities even if others have tried them and found them to be ineffective.

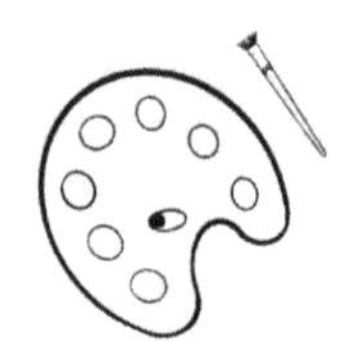

DISTRACT

Write examples of the DISTRACT skills.

D **Do something else that grabs your attention.**
Examples:

I **Imagine being somewhere else.**
Examples:

S **Use your 5 senses to distract you away from your pain.**
Examples:

T **Take a short vacation.**
Examples:

R **Read all types of books!**
Examples:

A **Do an arts and crafts project.**
Examples:

C **Contribute and do something nice for someone.**
Examples:

T **Keep your thoughts busy.**
Examples:

5 X 5 =
25

Adapted from Linehan, *DBT Skills Training Manual* (2015b)

7. WILLINGNESS AND WILLFULNESS

Willingness and willfulness are complete opposites. Willfulness is often explained first, and it is trying to control, avoid, or deny situations and other people. When kids are willful, they refuse to cooperate or only partially complete a task—on purpose. Of course, when asked about the partially completed task, they tend respond "I didn't know " or "I thought that was all I had to do." Willfulness is also holding a grudge against others.

Willingness is voluntarily responding to others and cooperating, without complaining or having a tantrum. It is fully participating in life, and at the very least, trying with a positive attitude.

Handout Directions

The handout begins the process of understanding the difference between willful and willing. Children and caregivers need to understand and notice the concepts first before discussing how to change from being willful to willing.

Described the qualities of willful and willing from the handout. Ask the child to observe and describe their own internal experience or "clues" of being willful and willing. When they experience being willful, ask them to describe the emotions, thoughts, body sensations, urges, and actions; repeat the same with willing. Write these on a whiteboard.

Point out the images of the bull and puppy on the handout. What are the characteristics of each? Do they represent willful or willing?

Discussion Questions

- When kids are willful or willing which road are they on? Rejecting or agreeing?
- Can a kid notice being willful or willing if they are not being mindful?
- Why does willful not work in life? Give an example
- Why does willing work in life? Give an example

Willingness & Willfulness

Willing is:

- *Being open.*
- *Accepting rules.*
- *Listening to others and their ideas.*
- *Obeying parents and teachers . . . even when you don't want to!*
- *Doing things without complaining, whining, or refusing.*
- *Responding from wise mind.*
- *Agreeing to try.*

Willing works!

Willful is:

- **Being closed.**
- **Refusing to do what you need to do . . . sitting on your hands.**
- **Ignoring problems.**
- **Responding from emotion mind.**
- **Giving up.**
- **Trying to change a situation through complaining, whining or temper tantrums.**
- **Refusing to try.**

Willful does not work!

Adapted from Linehan, DBT Skills Training Manual (2015b)

Worksheet Directions

The worksheet identifies the steps to change from being willful to willing. The steps have been adapted to be more concrete for a child's developmental level. As you describe the steps, refer back to the whiteboard notes obtained during the discussion of the willful and willing handout.

1. Notice I am being willful. Pay attention to my clues: feeling, thought, body sensation, and urge. For example, I am sad, think "I don't trust anyone," notice my throat hurts and it's hard to talk, and I have an urge to leave and go to sleep.
2. Make an agreement with myself to accept the things I think are unacceptable. For example, say, "I will accept the consequence even if I don't like it."
3. Do willing actions! Try half smile and willing hands. For example, I lean forward to fully listen, and make a half smile.

Suggestions for The Therapist

As you review the steps, help the children and caregivers connect the importance of mindfulness when they are being willing. If children do not notice their internal experience or "clues" (emotion, thought, body sensation, and urge), it will be more challenging for them to go from willful to willing.

Similar to other skills, it is helpful to role play a situation and the steps from willful to willing. Start with a general, more neutral situation, and then role play a situation that is more personally relevant to the child and caregiver.

From Willful

to Willing

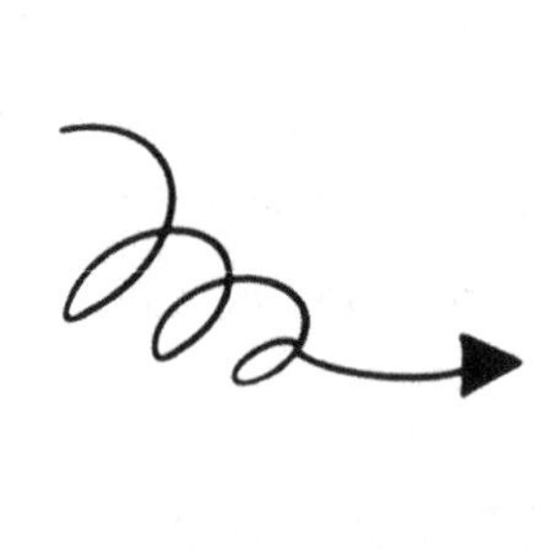

<u>Steps to Go From Willful to Willing</u>

1. Notice I am being willful. Pay attention to my clues: feeling, thought, body sensation, and urge. For example, I am mad, think "I don't care," notice my hands in a tight fist, and have an urge to throw things.

2 Make an agreement with myself to accept the things I think are unacceptable. For example, say, "I will accept it even if I don't like it."

3. Do willing actions! Try half smile and willing hands. For example, I lean forward to fully listen, and make a half smile.

Situation:

1. Notice I am being willful. Pay attention to my clues:

Feelings:

Thoughts:

Body sensations:

Urges:

2 Accept the things I think are unacceptable.

How did you do this?

3. Do a willing action! Try half smile and willing hands.

Describe your willing actions:

Adapted from Linehan, *DBT Skills Training Manual* (2015b)

8. PROS AND CONS

The pros and cons skill helps children to see that accepting a situation and tolerating pain will lead to a better outcome. Pros and cons is a useful skill to make a decision, and to resist harmful urges or behaviors when in emotion mind. When a child and caregiver make a pros and cons list, they write down the positive and negative outcomes of resisting impulsive behaviors and acting on impulsive behaviors. In making a pros and cons list, it is helpful to look at both short and long-term consequences.

"Pros and cons is a useful skill to make a decision, and to resist harmful urges or behaviors when in emotion mind."

How to make a pros and cons list:

1. Describe the decision or crisis behavior to examine.
2. Identify the advantages and disadvantages of the decision or behavior.
3. Decide if each pro and con has a short-term (ST) or long-term (LT) effect, it can also be both short and long-term.
4. As the child examines the completed list, can they make a wise mind decision?
5. When an upsetting urge hits, review the pros and cons list, and read the positive outcome of resisting the urge.

Handout Directions

When explaining the skill to the child and caregiver or children, it is essential to write out several pros and cons together. First, explain the skill.

Then, draw a grid on the whiteboard. Next, start with a less stressful decision, for example, the decision whether to use your "free pass" homework ticket or to hold on to it for a future time. Write the pros and cons in all four cells, and identify if they are short-term, long-term, or both outcomes. In looking at the completed sheet, can the child make a wise mind decision? Do other pros and cons lists using examples from the child and caregiver.

Discussion Questions

- Did you notice that pros and cons are like a dialectic?
- There are both pros and cons to decisions and behaviors. Do you agree?

Pros and cons is a skill for kids when they are deciding between two choices, or trying to fight back against a strong urge or hurtful behavior. The child can look at both sides, and make a wise mind decision that has a positive outcome.

How to make a pros and cons list:

1. Describe the decision or crisis behavior you want to figure out.
2. Identify the pros (+) and cons (-) of the decision or behavior.
3. Decide if each pro and con is a short-term (right now) or long-term (beyond today-next week, month, year) consequence or both.
4. Make a wise mind decision.
5. When an upsetting urge hits:
    - Review your pros and cons list, and read the positive outcome of resisting the urge.

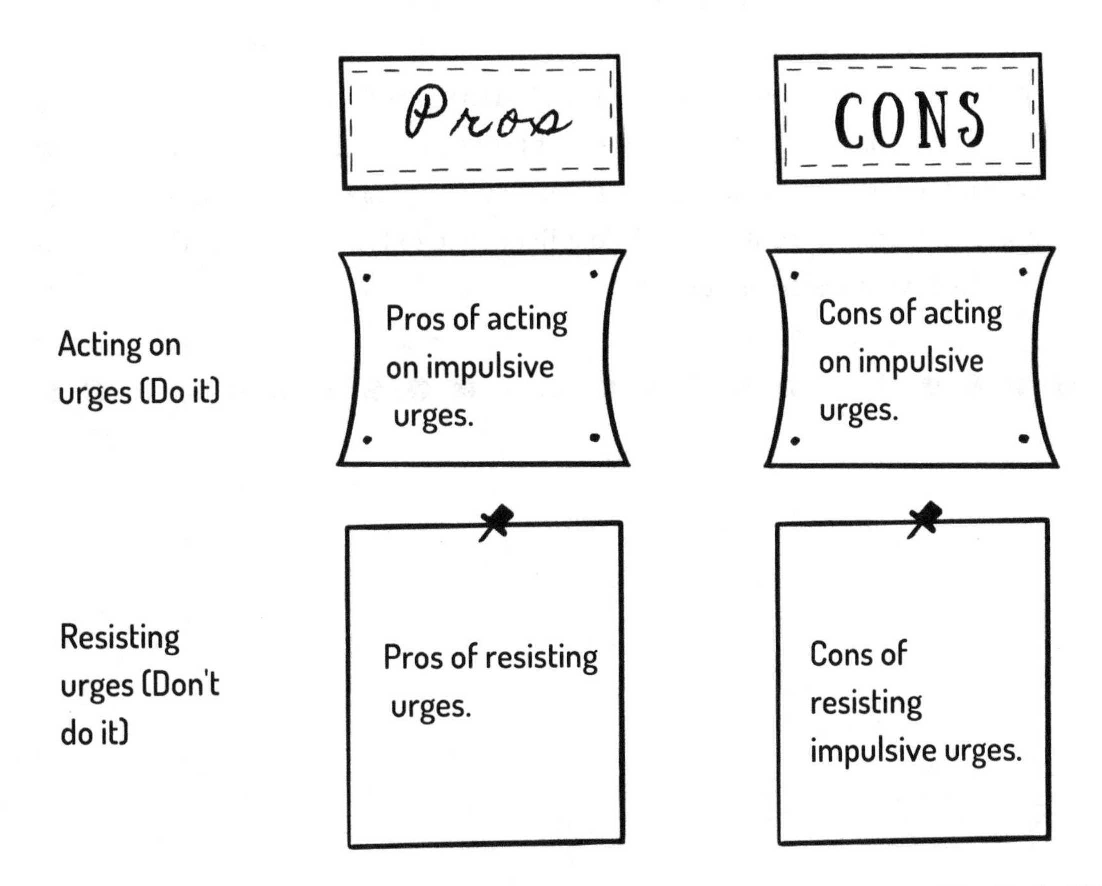

Adapted from Linehan, DBT Skills Training Manual (2015b)

Worksheet Directions

It is helpful to practice this worksheet in session, and to give it as a homework assignment. Ask the child to share a recent decision, or crisis behavior or urge. Together, fill in all four cells, adding if the pros and cons are short-term, long-term, or both.

Suggestions For The Therapist

This skill can also be used as a strategy with kids and caregivers who are stuck in power struggles over decisions and behaviors. As the child fills out the sheet, they can use their wise mind to make decisions leading to a positive outcome. When a caregiver hears their child's wise mind decision, it allows them to step back thus reducing opportunities for a power struggle. Of course, the child will need to follow through with the effective decision or behavior.

Pros and CONS

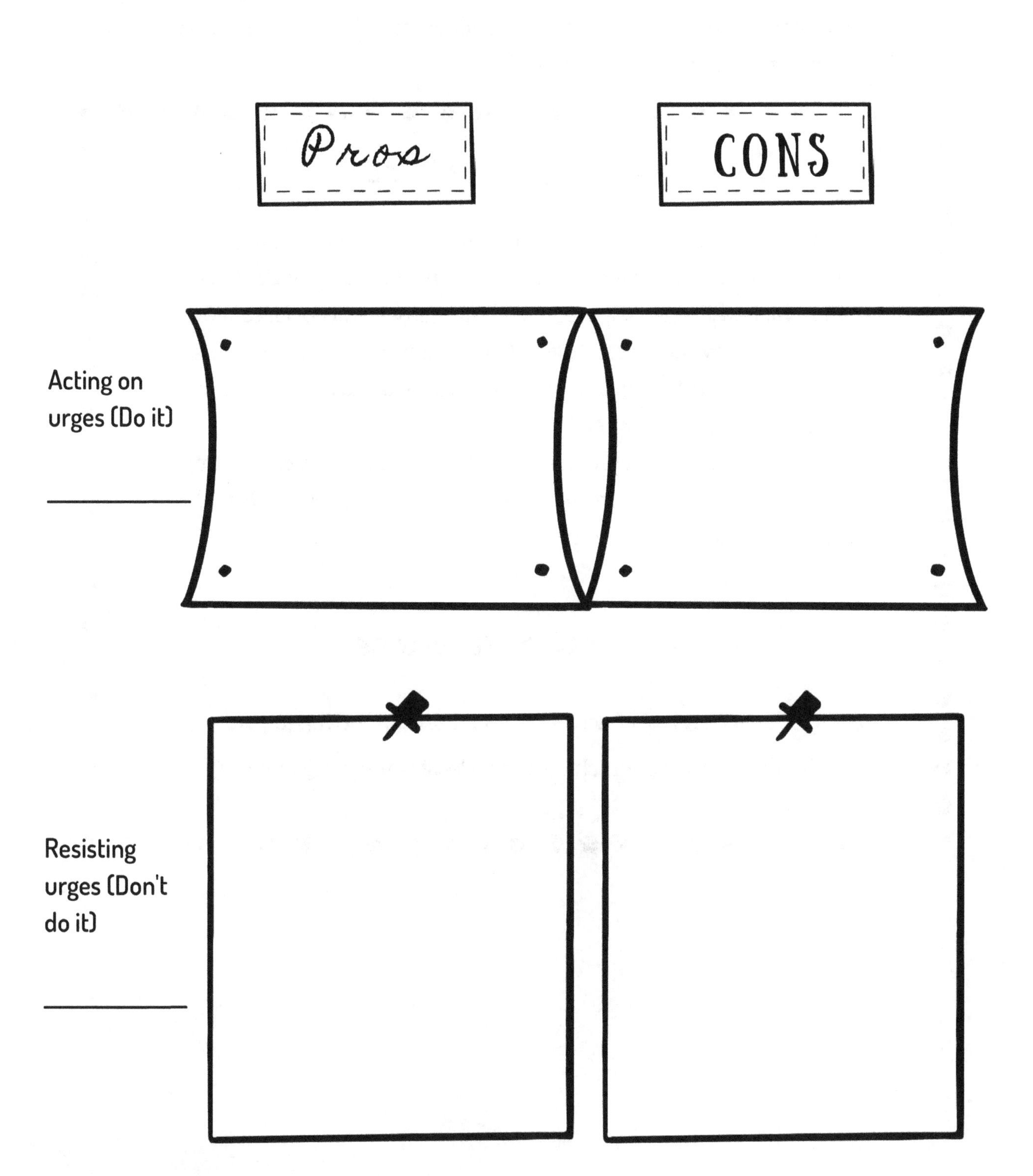

Adapted from Linehan, DBT Skills Training Manual (2015b)

9. SELF-SOOTHE

The self-soothe skills are a favorite of most kids; they enjoy having soft, nurturing objects to comfort themselves during times of distress. Self-soothe is using the five senses of touch, taste, smell, sound, and sight to soothe and comfort oneself.

Handout Directions

This is a fun skill to discuss with the child or group of kids. They have many interesting ideas which offers new and different suggestions to other children. Discuss self-soothe with five senses, and how it comforts kids when they feel upset. Give a few examples, "When I'm upset, I like to pet my fluffy dog" and "When I'm sad, I like to crawl under my favorite warm, soft blanket."

With the child and caregiver or children, brainstorm comforting, nurturing, kind ideas corresponding to each of the senses. Write the ideas under each heading on a whiteboard or handout.

Discussion Questions

- Of the five senses, which one(s) feel most comforting to you?
- Of the five senses, which one(s) feel least comforting to you?

Adapted from Linehan, *DBT Skills Training Manual* (2015b)

Worksheet Directions

Children can make a self-soothe box to keep in their bedroom, and the box will be ready for them when they need it. They can also make a small self-soothe kit to put in their backpack for aftercare, school, after school activities, camp, or other location.

This worksheet is to be assigned for homework. The children can list the items they placed in their self-soothe box for home, school, aftercare, after school activity, camp, or other location.

Suggestions for The Therapist

While most kids enjoy this skill, keep in mind that some experience the five senses in an annoying or aggravating way. Kids with sensory issues, find noise to be irritating; and children with an early history of neglect may not experience touch as soft or soothing.

dt

Items for my self-soothe box

Touch

Sound

Smell

Taste

Sight

My self soothe list
* My fluffy dog
* lavendar oil
* fruit gum
* flowers
* rain sounds

Adapted from Linehan, *DBT Skills Training Manual* (2015b)

SECTION 4

Emotion Regulation

The emotion regulation skills teach children how to understand their emotions, be less vulnerable to negative emotions, change unwanted emotions, and increase positive emotions. When children understand and implement the skills, they are better equipped to manage their emotions and avoid impulsive and problem behaviors such as, yelling, hitting, cussing, ignoring, refusing to talk, tantrums, overuse of electronics, refusing to go to school, cutting, and suicidality.

> "When children understand and implement the skills, they are better equipped to manage their emotions and avoid impulsive and problem behaviors . . ."

The activity book covers the traditional DBT-C skills of Emotion Wave, Surfing Your Emotion, Opposite Action, PLEASE skills, and LAUGH skills.

1. EMOTION WAVE

The emotion wave is a DBT-C skill adapted from the adult DBT model for describing emotions. It is important for children and caregivers to understand the cycle of emotions, and their transactional response to external and internal events. If the child can change one part of the cycle or wave, they can change their whole emotional response. The wave has six parts, let's look at each one to understand the emotion wave.

1. Event- the event starts the cycle in motion; it can be internal (thought, sensation) or external (a rude comment, being told "no").

2. Thoughts- the child's interpretation about the event; the meaning or story they tell themselves which is often based on learned beliefs and assumptions. Of course, assumptions and beliefs are not always correct, and this influences a child's feelings; this transaction is noted by the two-direction arrow.

3. Feelings- emotions cause an emotional reaction, and the child experiences changes in their face and body. For example, when nervous the child's body moves with active energy, such as finger or foot tapping. Sensations cannot be changed directly, rather are changed indirectly through distractions and activating the body's system of relaxing, such as TIP skills.

4. Action Urge- an urge is an internal experience, and the child has a strong desire to say or do something.

5. Action- when the child acts on the urge; they say or do something. Again, note the transaction between urge and action, shown by the two-direction arrow.

6. Aftereffects- consequences or outcomes that happen following an action and/or body reaction. For example, after being angry, the child feels tense and hypersensitive to other's behavior. Sometimes the aftereffects are a prompting event for the same or a new emotion causing the cycle to begin again as indicated by the arrow pointing back to Event.

Handout Directions

Describe the cycle of emotion or the emotion wave to the child and caregiver, or children. Then, choose a few examples to further illustrate the emotion wave such as the following vignettes.

1. A young child arrived home from school and her mom wasn't there. (Event) She thought mom must have been in a car accident and "Mom might die, and I can't take care of myself." (Thought) She feels scared, her heart begins to beat fast, and her stomach hurts. (Feelings) She feels like crying, and throwing up. (Action Urges) The little girl starts to scream for her mom, her body trembles, and she cries. (Action) She has trouble focusing, and remembers when mom was in a bad car accident a few months ago. (Aftereffects)
2. A boy asked his grandmother if he could go over to his friend's house. Grandma said, "No, not right now. We'll be eating dinner shortly." (Event) He thought, "Mimi is so mean; she never lets me do anything fun." (Thought) The boy is angry. He balls his hands into a fist, stomps on the floor, and feels his face get hot. (Feelings) The boy wants to push her and run out of the house to his friend's home. (Action Urges) He says, "You're rude! It's your fault I live here and not with mom!" He runs over to the door as if to open it, and starts to cry. (Actions) The boy feels numb, thinks about other times he was told "no," and times he spent with his mom who he misses greatly. (Aftereffects)

Discussion Questions

- What is the difference between the facts of an event and a person's interpretation of an event?
- Is it easy for kids to misunderstand a situation if they do not have enough information?
- How could the following situation be misunderstood? You walk into your classroom, and there are three girls talking together at their desks. As you enter the room, they all quit talking and look away from you.
- Take turns with the child and caregiver; use facial expressions and body posture to show different feelings. Try to guess which feeling the person is communicating.

Kids have to understand the cycle of emotion if they want to decrease emotional hurts, or stop or reduce unwanted feelings. Let's examine each component in the emotion wave:

4. **Action Urges**
A strong desire to say or do something.

↔

5. **Actions**
Doing a behavior or saying something.

3. **Feelings**
Emotional reactions, causes changes in the face and body.

↔

2. **Thoughts**
Your interpretation or meaning about the event.

6. **Aftereffects**
The outcomes that occur after your actions and/or body reactions.

←

1. **Event**
Something happens and starts the cycle.

Adapted from Linehan, *DBT Skills Training Manual*, 2015 (b)

Worksheet Directions

With the child and caregiver or as a group, practice several examples with the worksheet while in session. As a homework assignment, ask the child to complete the worksheet and describe one emotion wave.

Suggestions for The Therapist

This skill may be more difficult for children and caregivers who have not learned to identify and express emotions, or if they have been given negative feedback for expressing their emotion in the past.

Observe and describe one emotion wave from the week.

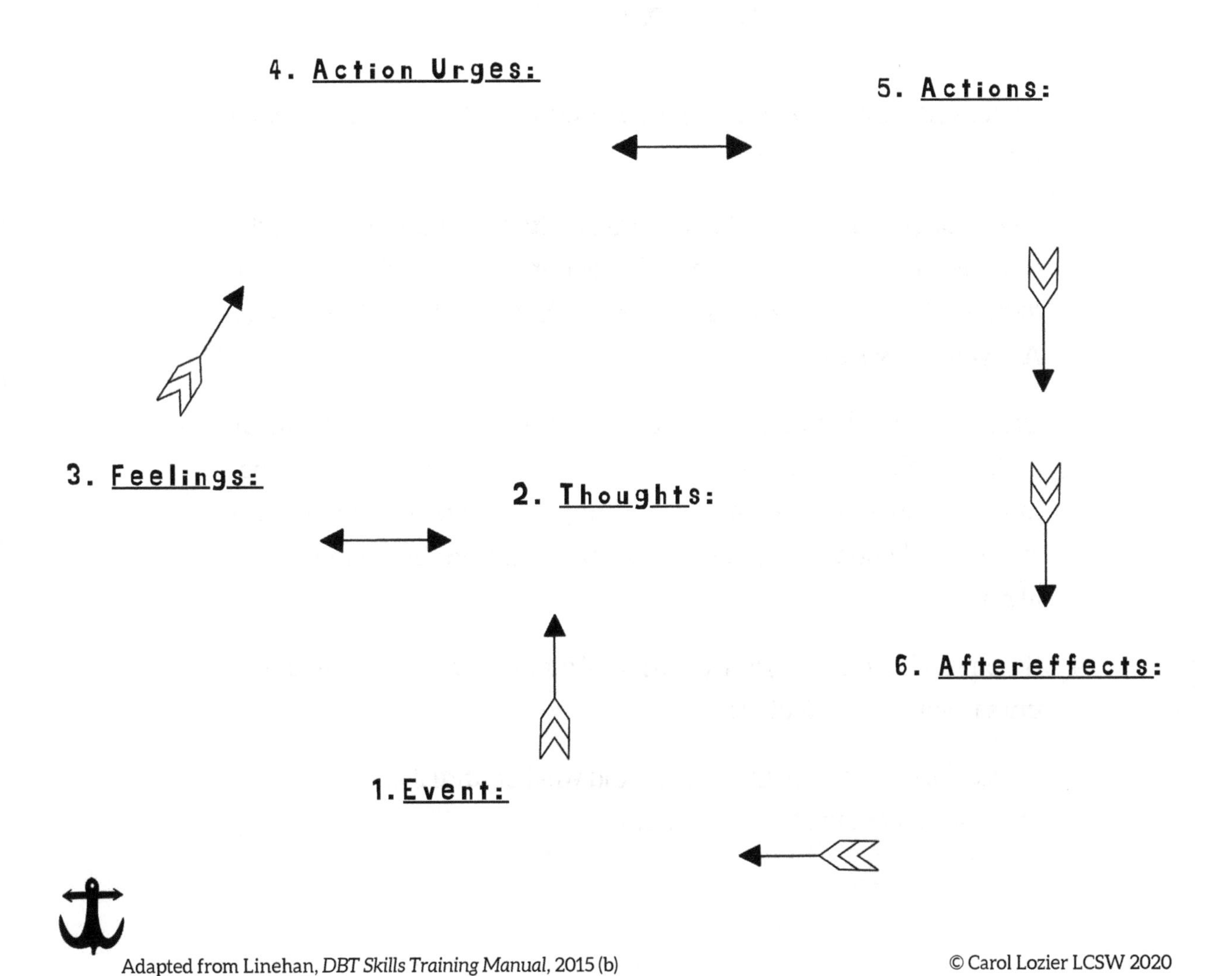

Adapted from Linehan, *DBT Skills Training Manual*, 2015 (b)

2. SURFING YOUR EMOTION

The surfing your emotion skill is derived from the adult DBT skill, letting go of emotional suffering. At times, painful emotions appear and feel like they will stick around forever. In actuality, emotions only last from seconds to minutes. Surfing your emotion teaches kids to mindfully observe their emotion without reacting to it, holding on to it, or judging it. When kids notice the emotion, coming and going like a wave, they can endure the feeling in a skillful way. Following are the steps to surfing your emotion:

"Surfing your emotion teaches kids to mindfully observe their emotion without reacting to it, holding on to it, or judging it."

1. Notice you are having a strong emotion; Observe it. Do not try to make it bigger or push it away

2. Take a step back; notice the emotion and its sensation in your body. Pay attention to the sensation and experience it as much as you can. Where is it? Is the sensation sharp or dull, hot or cold, numb, or tingly? Are your muscles tight or relaxed?

3. Notice the emotion coming and going like a wave. Imagine yourself on the beach, with the white sand and the waves coming and going. Imagine yourself on a surfboard riding the waves of emotion. Be curious and notice the emotion changing, moment by moment, just like a wave.

4. Become friends with your emotion. Accept it. Do not assume it is unreasonable or ridiculous.

5. Notice the emotion getting weaker and weaker until it goes away just like waves flowing back into the sea.

Handout Directions

Discuss the goal of surfing your emotion is to observe a strong emotion without avoiding it, holding on to it, or getting rid of it. Inform the child and caregiver or group members that emotions last from seconds to minutes, and surfing the emotion helps them to tolerate it skillfully. Explain the steps, and the importance of being mindful and curious as they surf their emotion.

Discussion Questions

- When you experience a strong emotion do you avoid it, reject it, push it away, or hold on to it?
- Emotions last from seconds to minutes. What do you think about this truth?
- What do you think about the idea of being friends with your emotion?

Surfing Your Emotion

Surfing is observing your emotion without reacting to it or acting on it. Remember, the emotion won't last forever, from seconds to minutes. Following are the steps to surfing your emotion:

1. Notice you are having a strong emotion. Observe it.

2. Take a step back; notice your emotion and it's sensation in your body. Where is it in your body? Is the sensation hot, cold, tingly, or tight?

3. Notice the emotion coming and going like a wave. Imagine yourself at the beach sitting on the white sand; riding the waves of emotion on a surf board. Be curious and notice it changing, coming in and going out, just like a wave.

4. Become friends with your emotion. Accept it; don't assume it's unreasonable or ridiculous.

5. Notice the emotion getting weaker and weaker until it goes away, just like waves flowing back into the sea.

Adapted from Linehan, *DBT Skills Training Manual*, 2015 (b)

Worksheet Directions

As you practice surfing your emotion with the child and caregiver, or children, continue to remind them to be mindful at each step. Ask them to observe their emotion and body sensations in the moment, and in a nonjudgmental way.

Suggestions for The Therapist

For children who are younger or more visual, ask them to draw a picture of themselves surfing the emotion. Encourage the child to be creative as she draws her picture. Allow the child to share her drawing with others.

Ask the children to draw a picture or write a note to their emotion and ask it to become friends with them.

Describe one example of surfing your emotion.

Situation:

1. Notice you are having a strong emotion. Describe it:

2. Take a step back; notice the emotion and it's sensation in your body. Describe the sensation:

3. Imagine yourself on a surf board riding the waves of emotion. Stay curious, and notice it's changes, coming and going. Draw what you imagine on the back of this page.

4. Become friends with the emotion; accept it. What would you say to the emotion?

5. Notice your emotion getting weaker and weaker. Do you notice them going away?

Adapted from Linehan, *DBT Skills Training Manual*, 2015 (b)

3. OPPOSITE ACTION

Opposite action is changing an emotion by acting opposite to the action urge. Opposite action is effective when the child understands the facts of a situation and is still not able to lower their emotion. For example, a child knows her foster mom plans to pick her up today after school, just like every day over the past year. All day long, the child worries that her foster mom will not show up, and that she will be taken to a new foster home.

"Opposite action is effective when the child understands the facts of a situation and is still not able to lower their emotion."

Sometimes the facts do fit the situation, but the intensity and duration of the emotion is not effective in meeting the child's goals. As an example, dad is driving his son home from school. The son wants to stop and get a fast food meal. Dad says "no" as they will have a snack at home. The child begins to yell, "You're the worst dad ever. I hate you!" as he kicks the back of the seat; this continues all the way home and then for an additional forty-five minutes until he finally calms.

Opposite action is also effective when a child is avoiding things that need to be done. For example, a boy is anxious about incorrectly answering homework questions on his school papers. So, he completes homework assignments but does not turn them in. In another situation, a girl feels anxious whenever she has a substitute teacher at school. She avoids going to class by telling the teacher she is sick and goes home for the day.

The steps to opposite action include:

1. Name your current emotion.
2. What is the urge that goes with the emotion? What do I want to say or do?
3. Ask yourself, "Is this an emotion I want to change?" If yes, continue on!

4. Figure out the opposite action.
5. Do the opposite action; do it all the way including your tone of voice, facial expression, and body posture.
6. Keep doing opposite action until the emotion lessens.

"Opposite action is also effective when a child is avoiding things that need to be done."

In figuring out an opposite action, it is necessary to do it all the way. When kids first learn this skill they often guess, stopping the behavior, which is not the opposite action. In teaching this skill it helps to first name your action urge, and then identify the opposite action. Do not forget to include the opposite tone of voice, facial expression, and body posture. Using the last example above, the girl's action urge is to leave class. The opposite behavior is to remain in class with a confident voice, sitting tall, raising her hand and fully participating in class.

Handout Directions

Explain opposite action and describe the steps of the skill. Once you review the skill and its steps, discuss how to determine the opposite action. It will be necessary to go through quite a few examples before the kids can name the full opposite action instead of a partial one.

Discussion Questions

- What opposite pictures do you see on the page?
- Who can define "action urge?"
- What are the action urges that go with the emotions fear, happy, sad, angry, love, guilt, and jealous?
- From the list we created, what is the opposite action of each item on the list of action urges?
- Does anyone think doing an opposite action is phony? Explain your answer.
- Does the opposite action help your emotion decrease? Is this the goal of opposite action?

Opposite action is changing your behavior by acting opposite to your urge-- which decreases your emotion. Following are the steps to opposite action:

1. Name your current emotion.
2. What is the urge that goes with the emotion? What do I want to say or do?
3. Ask yourself, "Is this an emotion I want to change?" If yes, continue on!
4. Figure out the opposite action.
5. Do the opposite action; do it all the way including your tone of voice, facial expression, and body posture.
6. Keep doing opposite action until your emotion lessens.

Some examples of emotion and it's opposite action are:

Scared/Nervous: Act brave and do it! (As long as there's no danger)

Sad/Depressed: Get active; get moving!

Angry/Frustrated: Be respectful; Take breaths and calm- stay away from the person until you are calm.

Guilt: Take responsiblity for your part and apologize.

Adapted from Linehan, *DBT Skills Training Manual* (2015b)

Worksheet Directions

This is a skill that is fun for kids to learn and practice. Use various vignettes to practice with the child and caregiver, or group of children. Read a vignette, discuss each step, and then role play showing a full opposite action. Remind the kids to use a matching facial expression, body posture, and tone of voice to the opposite action.

Suggestions for The Therapist

At times, an initial concern for people is the idea that opposite action is being "phony." If this question arises, talk about the differences between being phony and being effective. Also note that opposite action will decrease the emotion while being phony will not.

Emotions and their opposite action:
Scared/Nervous .... Act brave and do it! (As long as there's no danger)
Sad/Depressed.....................................Get active; get moving!
Angry/Frustrated.................................Be respectful; Stay away from the person until you are calm.
Guilt...Take responsiblity for your part and apologize.

Situation:

1. Name your current emotion:

2. What is the urge that goes with my emotion? What do I want to say or do?

3. Ask yourself, "Is this an emotion I want to change?" (If yes, continue on!)

4. Figure out the opposite action; name it:

5. Do the opposite action; do it all the way including tone of voice, facial expression, and body posture.

6. Keep doing the opposite action until your emotion decreases.

Adapted from Linehan, *DBT Skills Training Manual* (2015b)

4. PLEASE SKILLS

The PLEASE skills reduce a child's vulnerability to emotion mind. When a child's body is out of balance from a lack of sleep, hunger, illness, or exercise they have a harder time managing their emotions. When kids have not eaten for several hours, they are quick to say they are hungry; they may be irritable and whine, "I need something to eat–I'm hangry!"

The PLEASE skills are an acronym and each letter communicates the following meaning.

PL-Physical Illness: When kids do not feel well, they are more likely to experience negative emotions. When kids are sick, they need to see a doctor. They need to take their medicines as prescribed as missing even a dose or two can cause havoc on their emotions.

E-Eat balanced: What kids eat directly affects their mood, positively or negatively. Eating regular meals and snacks around the same time everyday helps keep a stable mood; skipping meals can cause a negative mood. Healthy foods like fruit, vegetables, whole grains, and lean proteins help to improve mood while sugar and junk food cause low energy and mood.

A-Avoid drugs that are not prescribed by your doctor: Alcohol and non-prescribed drugs are bad for kids. The therapist will have to decide if they want to go into more detail for this skill or just keep it simple, some of this may depend on the child's age or environment.

S-Balance sleep: A lack of sleep or disrupted sleep causes a negative mood–a "cranky" child. From the ages of 6 to 12, children require 9 -12 hours of sleep. Sleep routines can aid in inducing restful sleep as well as putting all electronics away 30 minutes prior to bedtime.

E-Exercise: Exercise can improve a child's mood. Children need to exercise for 20 minutes, 5 - 7 times a week. Aerobic exercise can be fun! Some examples are: tag, jump rope, dodge ball, jumping on the trampoline, soccer, gymnastics, ice skating, four square, kick ball, tae kwon do, field hockey, volleyball and many others. Encourage kids to find and keep doing exercises that are fun for them.

Handout Directions

While these concepts are not difficult for kids to grasp, they may not have ever made the connection to their mood. Discuss each letter, its meaning, and how it influences mood in a positive or negative way.

Discussion Questions

- When you are sick, have you noticed your emotion changes? Explain your answer.
- If you miss one to two doses of medicine how does it affect your emotions? (If the child takes medicine)
- What foods make you feel bad? (Have a negative emotion.)
- What foods make you feel good? (Have a positive or stable emotion)
- What happens to your emotions when you do not sleep enough? Or when you sleep too much?
- What is your bedtime routine (sleep habits)?
- Do you feel better after exercising?
- Name aerobic exercises that are fun to you.
- Name a few exercises you would be willing to try.

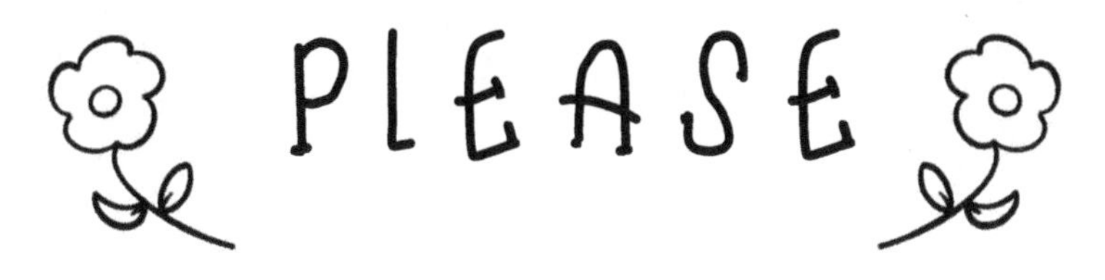

When a child's body is out of balance, they are more sensitive to emotion mind. So when the child is tired, hungry, sick or has missed their medicine, they have a harder time staying in charge of their feelings.

PL Physical Illness. When kids are sick, they feel bad--physically and emotionally. They need to see the doctor when they are sick, and take medicine as the doctor prescribes it. Missing their medicine, even one or two times, can cause negative emotions.

E Eat balanced. When kids don't eat they feel sluggish, and are more likely to have a negative emotion--some kids call this "hangry." Kids need to eat the right amount of healthy food for their body to grow, and to keep a positive mood. Typically, kids need 3 meals and 2 snacks each day.

A Avoid drugs not prescribed by your doctor. The only drug kids should take are ones prescribed by their doctor. Any other drugs or alcohol are bad for your body and emotions.

ZZZZZ...

S Balance sleep. It's hard to stay in control of your emotions when you're tired, without regular sleep most kids feel "cranky." Children, age 6 to 12, need 9 to 12 hours of sleep. Keep a bedtime routine to help you sleep better. Put up all electronics at least 30 minutes before bedtime.

E Exercise. Exercise is fun, and it gives kids positive emotions. Have a goal to exercise 5 - 7 days per week for 20 minutes. Find an aerobic activity that you enjoy like soccer, hopscotch, dodge ball, tennis, football, jump rope, basketball, four square, running, gymnastics, jumping on a trampoline, and horseback riding.

Adapted from Linehan, *DBT Skills Training Manual* (2015b)

Worksheet Directions

This worksheet is homework for the child and caregiver, or children. Over the week, they will keep daily track of their PLEASE skills. In the first three columns, they will answer yes or no if they took their prescribed medicines, ate balanced amounts of healthy foods, and avoided non-prescribed drugs. The fourth column records the number of hours of sleep, and the final column notes the type of exercise and amount of time exercised.

Suggestions for The Therapist

Spend some time talking about healthy foods, exercise, and sleep habits that the kids have already incorporated into their life. In a group it is especially meaningful for the practitioner to write group members answers on a white board for everyone to see. Sometimes, seeing what the other kids are doing has a positive impact on the rest of the group. Also, ask what healthy foods, exercise, and sleep habits the kids are willing to try and possibly incorporate into their daily life.

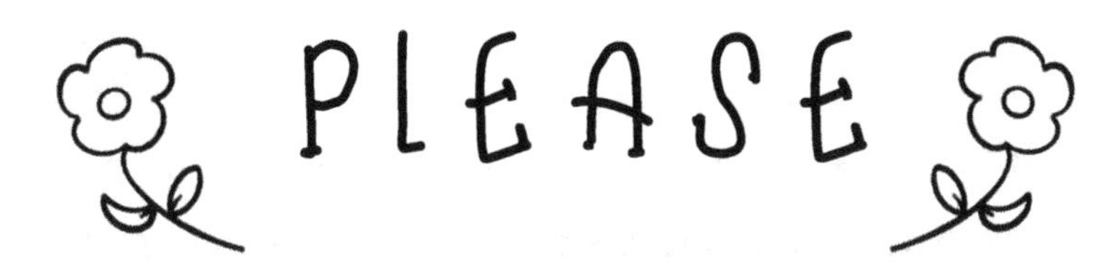

Over the week, use the chart to maintain your physical health and emotions. Write yes or no, in the following columns: did you take your prescribed medicine, eat balanced, and avoid drugs?
In the column, balance sleep, write the number of hours you slept.
In the last column, name the aerobic exercise and amount of time you exercised; the goal is 20 minutes, 5-7 times this week.

Day of the week	Rx Medicine	Balance Eating	Avoid Drugs	Balance Sleep	Exercise
MON					
TUES					
WED					
THURS					
FRI					
SAT					
SUN					

ZZZZZ...

Adapted from Linehan, *DBT Skills Training Manual* (2015b)

5. LAUGH SKILLS

The LAUGH skills, which are derived from the DBT adult skills ABC, increase positive emotions. Like other skills, this one is an acronym, and each letter stands for a different skill.

L-Let go of worries! We do not want kids to ruin their positive experience by focusing on their worries. We also do not want them to worry about when the positive experience will end, or if they deserve it as this takes away from the positive experience too. Children need to remain focused on the positive experience, and be a mindful participant in it.

A-Apply yourself. Do challenging activities. When kids complete these activities, they feel more confident, competent, and believe in themselves. When they complete an activity, challenge them to go to the next level. There are many types of activities for kids from hobbies to sports to helping with chores around the house.

U-Use cope ahead skill. Plan ahead and effectively manage problem situations. Encourage the child to plan ahead using skillful ways to cope with an upsetting or unpleasant situation. Also, in stressful situations, kids may forget what they want to say. Ask the child to decide which DBT skills to use, and to practice them alone or in a role play with their caregiver or therapist.

G-Set goals. When kids have clear goals, they make a life built on their own values, creating a life with positive experiences and emotions. It is important for kids to identify their own values and goals, and not just follow others. Values are extremely important to children as they give them a life direction and act as a guide in decision making. A kids values list will follow the worksheet; the list will provide ideas for the kids to consider as they identify their own values list.

The therapist will need to explain to the child and caregiver how to take small steps in reaching the goals. Once the child determines a goal, she will need to identify objectives or small, incremental steps to reach the goal. Make sure the objectives are reasonable and can be met by the child in a realistic time frame. The therapist and/or caregiver will help the child to identify the goals and objectives.

H-Have fun! Kids need to have lots of fun events in their life. Fun experiences create positive emotions. Have at least one fun experience every day.

Handout Directions

Explain the LAUGH skills and its goal to the child and caregiver, or children. Describe each of the LAUGH skills, and how each one can create positive experiences and feelings for the child. As you describe each one, allow the child to share any positive experience that has already occurred in the child's life. This information will be valuable as the child and caregiver prepare for the worksheet.

Discussion Questions

- Have your worries ever gotten in the way of a fun experience?
- What DBT skills can you use to refocus on a positive experience if you begin to worry?
- Have you developed an ability or competency in any hobby or activity? Explain your answer.
- How does it feel to have developed an ability?
- Look at the kids values list. What top 5 values would you choose to have as goals in your life?
- What is one value and goal that you would like to work on first?
- What is one small step you can take toward your identified goal?
- What are some fun experiences you have had? Name big ones and small ones.
- What are some fun things you would like to do that you have not done before?

LAUGH

Create positive emotions.

Worries

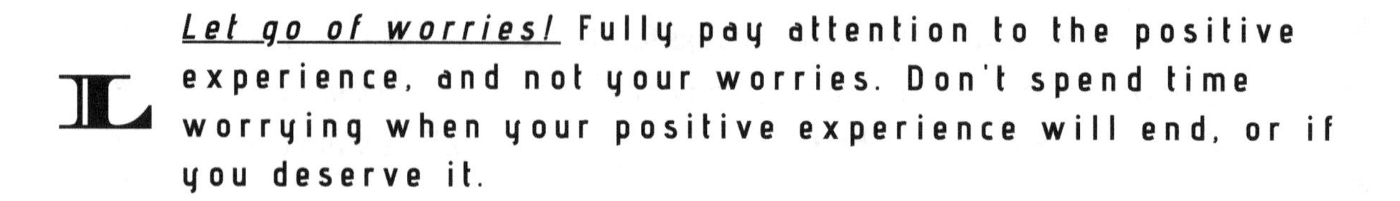

L — *Let go of worries!* Fully pay attention to the positive experience, and not your worries. Don't spend time worrying when your positive experience will end, or if you deserve it.

A — *Apply yourself.* Do challenging activities. When you complete these activities, you will feel more confident, and believe-- *I can do it!* Once you have finished an activity, challenge yourself to go to the next level.

U — *Use cope ahead skill* Figure out ways to deal with problem situations; plan ahead how you will cope with it. Decide which DBT skills to use, and practice them by yourself or out loud with someone else.

G — *Set goals.* Work toward goals that are based on your values to have more positive experiences and emotions. Don't just follow other's goals.

H — *Have fun!* Participate in fun events in life; they create positive emotions. Have at least one fun experience everyday.

fun

Adapted from Linehan, *DBT Skills Training Manual*, 2015 (b)

Worksheet Directions

As mentioned, the LAUGH skills are a combination of the adult DBT skills, ABC. The LAUGH skills encompass a great deal of information and skills. As a result, they can be learned over a period of time rather than just one week. As a homework assignment, choose one or possibly two skills to work on with the child and caregiver.

Suggestions for The Therapist

The apply yourself skill is derived from the adult DBT skill, build mastery. In this skill the therapist encourages the child to choose an activity that is a bit of a challenge—not too much and not too little. When the child succeeds in a challenging task, they feel accomplished which gives them feelings of competence and mastery. Once they complete a task, encourage them to strive for the next difficult step.

In goal setting, the child will require adult assistance to identify goals based on their values. Then, they will choose one goal and determine the steps to reach that goal. Without adult help, the child may not be able to pinpoint the small steps needed to reach the identified goal.

LAUGH

Practice LAUGH skills to create positive emotions

L <u>*Let go of worries!*</u>

I paid attention to my positive experience and not my worries:

A <u>*Apply yourself.*</u>

I completed this activity:

My next challenge is:

U <u>*Use cope ahead skill*</u>

An upcoming stressful situation is:

My plan to cope ahead is:

G <u>*Set goals.*</u>

One of my values is:

A goal, based on my values, is:

The first, small step toward my goal is:

H <u>*Have fun!*</u>

My fun experience was:

Adapted from Linehan, *DBT Skills Training Manual*, 2015 (b)

5A. Kids Values List

The kids values list coordinates with the "G-goals" skill of the LAUGH skills. The kids values list provides a number of ideas for children to consider as they identify their own personal list of values. Explain each value with the child and caregiver, or with the group of children.

"The kids values list provides a number of ideas for children to consider as they identify their own personal list of values."

Ask the children to identify their top five most important values, and encourage them to share their thoughts with others. These ideas will be used in their LAUGH skills worksheet page when they begin to identify their goals and objectives.

Kids Values List

Page 1

Be in relationships- work on relationships with family and friends, begin new relationships, give and receive affection and love, create an inner circle of close relationships.

Hopefulness- overcome painful problems and see them as an opportunity to grow, rise above disappointments and believe things will turn out for the best.

Self-respect- keep boundaries to say "no" when it's needed, accept when others say "no," be a leader who has positive goals.

Trustworthy- following through with your commitments to the best of your ability, and be reliable.

Honest- tell the truth at all times, don't exaggerate or leave out important information.

Hard Work- name goals, work hard to achieve goals, get chores and school work done, make good grades, be determined to get through hard times and keep going until you achieve your goal.

Creativity- discover your creative interests and have fun with them, try new hobbies, use your creative interests to share your thoughts and feelings.

Learn- be a curious kid at school and in life, be open to learning new things, read, and study.

Build character- be kind and caring; be loyal and keep your word, be willing to forgive others, and be brave in everyday life.

Adapted from Linehan, *DBT Skills Training Manual* (2015b)

Kids Values List

Page 2

Respect yourself and others- be a humble kid (don't brag), follow the rules, treat others with respect too.

Forgiveness- be willing to forgive yourself and others, repair relationships when there's been a problem, give a sincere apology, and don't hold a grudge.

Have fun- make time for fun activities and experiences, play with family and friends, participate in fun activities at school and in the community.

Physically fit- take care of your body; exercise, have balanced sleep, and keep a healthy diet.

Contribute to others- help those in need, volunteer, belong to a group whose goal is to improve the community.

Gratitude- be thankful even when things are hard, look on the bright side. . . what have I gained from this experience even if I didn't ask for it?

Other-

SECTION 5

Interpersonal Effectiveness

The fourth module of DBT-C is interpersonal effectiveness. This module or group of skills teaches the child to get along better with others, repair relationship problems, and to encourage themselves during times of hopelessness.

"... get along better with others, repair relationship problems, and to encourage themselves during times of hopelessness."

The activity book covers the traditional DBT-C skills of cheerleading, DEAR skills, and FRIEND skills. It also includes the skill, repairs.

1. REPAIRS

When children have dysregulated moods, they may face more difficulties in their relationships due to irritability and impulsive behaviors. Relationship mistakes occur for everyone whether they are intentional or purely by mistake. Either way, children need to learn how to apologize for any pain they cause to others.

"Relationship mistakes occur for everyone whether they are intentional or purely by mistake."

A repair, or apology, is an interpersonal effectiveness skill to build and keep good relationships. When a child apologizes, he is acknowledging to the other person that he caused them a hurt, he respects them and the friendship, and he wants to make amends.

The repair skill is comprised of the following five steps.

1. When a child starts the repair, they call the person by name. This shows the person respect and that the child is serious about correcting and healing the situation.

2. The child takes responsibility for their wrongdoing or mistake. They identify specific behavior that caused the other person pain, and they say, "I am sorry for . . ."

3. Next, the child asks the other person for forgiveness, "Can you forgive me?"

4. The child validates the other person's answer, even if they do not like it or agree with it. The other person may immediately accept the child's apology, or they may want to take some time to think about it. If the other person is not ready, the child needs to validate their feelings or concerns.

5. Now, the child needs to do things differently. In order for the child to demonstrate a full apology, they need to show different or new behavior. An apology without behavior change is not complete, and not as meaningful to the other person. People are reluctant to accept future apologies for repetitive behavior.

Handout Directions

Describe the repair skill to the child or children; explain each step. This is an important skill for children to maintain relationships over a period of time. It is an effective skill for children to have and use throughout their lifetime.

Discussion Questions

- Have you ever hurt a friend's feelings either by mistake or on purpose? Explain your answer.
- How did you feel when your friend told you they felt sad or hurt?
- What do you think is the hardest part of making a repair?
- What skills can you use when it is hard to make the repair?
- How do you feel when a person apologizes, but keeps doing the same hurtful behavior over and over? Do you want to continue to accept their apology?

Repair

skills to keep a relationship

All kids make mistakes. After all, how could they learn to do things better if they never messed up in the first place? The repair skill was created for this purpose!
Let's look at how to repair relationships when you make mistakes . . . whether by accident or on purpose.

1. When you begin, call the person by name. This shows the person that you respect them, and are serious about correcting the situation.

2. Be specific as you take responsibility for your wrongdoing or mistake. Start your sentence with, "I am sorry for . . ."

3. Ask the other person for forgiveness, "Can you forgive me?"

4. Validate their answer, even if you don't like it. The other person may immediately accept your apology, or they may need some time to think about it. If they aren't ready, validate their feelings or concerns. Remember to show good eye contact!

5. Do things differently. In order to make a full apology, you need to show you are behaving in a new way. An apology without a behavior change isn't a complete one. People may not want to accept future apologies for the same behavior.

Worksheet Directions

Use the worksheet to guide the child and caregiver, or group of children, in writing a repair. After the repair is written, encourage the child to read it aloud, and then role play repairing with the intended person.

Suggestions for The Therapist

Before discussing the repair skill, the therapist may need to review the validation skill with the children which is found in Section 1: What is DBT?

Repair

skills to keep a relationship

Write a repair; use the sentence starters and questions below to help you.

Dear ______________________________,

I am sorry for: (be specific)

Will you forgive me?

Thank you for forgiving me, OR
I understand you're not ready to forgive me yet;
it makes sense to me because:

From,
(Your name)_______________

(Remember: An apology without behavior change isn't complete.)
I plan to--OR--I have been doing these things differently:

Adapted from Lozier, *DBT Therapeutic Activity Ideas for Working with Teens (2018)*

2. FRIEND SKILLS

The DBT-C FRIEND skills are a combination of the adult DBT skills MAN, GIVE, and FAST. The FRIEND skills help children to get along better with others, and like other DBT skills, it is an acronym. Each letter has a meaning, and they are described below.

F-Be fair to yourself and the other person. In relationships, children need to balance considering themselves and others. When a child is being fair to others, it boosts their self-respect. When the child disregards the other person, it causes them to have negative feelings and lower self-respect. In being fair children need to maintain a balance of staying true to their own beliefs and wishes, and honoring the other person's too.

R-Respect the other person. When children are nice, kind, and respectful instead of aggressive it shows respect to the other person. This means a relationship without attacks, judging, disrespect, and threats; in other words, no aggressive words or actions.

I-Act interested in the other person. Children have to show interest in other people if they want others to show interested in them. In showing interest, the child listens without interrupting, and waits patiently if the other person prefers to talk at a later time. Children must act interested even when they do not feel like it in order to remain effective in the relationship.

E-Use an easy manner. Create a comfortable, low stress environment with others. Children can be lighthearted in the relationship, and show an easy manner with their facial expression, body posture, and tone of voice. They can smile and use humor, and avoid demanding, controlling behavior.

N-Negotiate. When children negotiate, they are showing balance in the relationship. Negotiating is a willingness to give something to the other person so that they may get something in return. In some situations, the child may have to change their offer to find common ground with the other person.

D-Be direct. In an interaction, the child stays focused on their goal without getting distracted by other topics. Distractions may be another subject from the past, or another issue that is brought up in response to the current discussion. In the interaction, the child shows confidence in his tone of voice, body posture, and facial expression.

Handout Directions

Explain to the child and caregiver, or the group of children, that the goal of the FRIEND skill is to get along better with others. This skill is an acronym; describe each letter and its meaning. Use the questions below to further the discussion.

Discussion Questions

- How does it feel to you when others aren't being fair?
- How does it make you feel when others judge, threaten, or attack you? Do you want to be in a relationship with them?
- What is the difference between *acting* interested and *being* interested? Can you act interested even when you are not interested in the discussion?
- Give an example of a time you negotiated with someone.
- Show a confident body posture, facial expression, and tone of voice.

Skills to get along with others

F

Be fair to yourself and others.
Stay balanced in being fair to both yourself and the other person.

r

Respect the other person.
Show respect; be gentle and nice. Don't verbally attack or judge others. Pay attention to your tone of voice and facial expression too!

i

Act Interested in the other person. Keep eye contact and remember not to interrupt others when they are talking.

e

Use an Easy manner.
Smile and use a little humor. Remember not to give the other person a negative attitude.

n

50/50

Negotiate.
Be willing to give a little in order to get something in return. Be open, ask and offer other solutions or ideas.

d

Be direct.
Act confident. Stay focused on your goals without getting distracted by another topic; "Let's come back to that after we finish this discussion."

Worksheet Directions

This worksheet can be assigned for homework, and also used in session. If possible, allow the child or children to experience these skills by role playing several situations. Pair the children into groups of two, or pair the child with the therapist or caregiver. Invite one child to talk about any subject of their choice and the other person, the listener, will first act interested and then act disinterested. Ask the child which scenario he preferred: the listener who acted interested or disinterested?

Suggestions For The Therapist

Remind the children to remain mindful in these skills so that they are most effective. It is challenging to stay focused on a topic, act confident, act interested and so on if the child is multi-tasking, or having judgmental thoughts about themselves or others.

Skills to get along with others

Choose a situation to practice the FRIEND skill. Describe how you used the skill.

F I was fair to myself and the other person:

r I remained gentle and nice, and respectful:

i I acted interest in the other person:

e I Smiled and used a little humor:

n I negotiated; my idea was:

d I acted confident, and stay focused on my goal:

Adapted from Linehan, *DBT Skills Training Manual*, 2015 (b)

3. DEAR SKILLS

The DEAR skills teach children how to ask for something, say "no" clearly, or maintain their point of view. Often times, children are too aggressive or compliant in asking for their needs to be met; the DEAR skills help them to skillfully ask for what they need in relationships. The skills provide children a structure for how to achieve their goals in a discussion. The DEAR skills, an acronym, are explained as follows below.

"Often times, children are too aggressive or compliant in asking for their needs to be met . . ."

D: Describe the situation. Begin by describing the facts of the situation without judgment. This is like using the mindfulness skill, describe. The child is describing what they observe in the situation.

E: Express feelings and opinions. In this step, the children share their thoughts and feelings in a clear manner. They cannot expect people to know what they are thinking if they do not clearly and verbally express themselves.

A: Assert yourself by asking for what you need or saying no when it is needed. In this next step, the children ask for what they want, or say "no" in a clear way. It is not effective for the child to avoid asking for what they need in a relationship, and on the other hand they cannot be bossy, telling others what to do.

R: Reinforce or reward the person ahead of time. Children tell the other person the reward or positive thing that will happen if they agree to the child's request. The child lets the person know how it will help her or him, the child, or the situation improve.

Handout Directions

Describe the DEAR skills to the child and caregiver, or children. Inform them the goal of the skills are to ask for what they want or need, or to clearly say "no" to others. Teach them each letter of the skill, and describe the meaning of each letter.

Discussion Questions

- Is it hard to ask for what you need? Do you tend to act aggressive or passive in asking for what you want?
- Do you ever avoid asking for what you need?
- What is the difference between asking for what you want and demanding it?
- Do you think it motivates people if you reward them for agreeing to your request?

DEAR

Skills to ask for something, or say no in a relationship.

DESCRIBE YOUR SITUATION.

Begin by describing what you observe in the situation; this is the same as the mindfulness skill of describing. Stick to the facts of the situation.

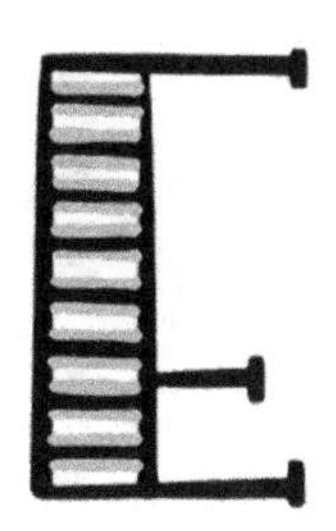

EXPRESS YOUR FEELINGS AND OPINIONS

Express how you feel, and what you believe about the situation. Be clear; don't expect the other person to already know how you think and feel about it.

ASSERT YOURSELF BY ASKING FOR WHAT YOU NEED OR SAYING NO WHEN IT'S NEEDED

Let others know what you need from them, or clearly tell them no. Don't avoid asking for what you need, and don't tell other people what they should do.

REINFORCE OR REWARD THE PERSON AHEAD OF TIME

Let the other person know the reward or positive thing that will happen if they accept your request, or your reply of "no." Tell the other person how it will help them, you, or the situation improve.

Adapted from Linehan, *DBT Skills Training Manual*, 2015 (b)

Worksheet Directions

The DEAR skills present a structured way for children to ask for what they need, say no, or maintain their point of view. Even with this structure, children may need additional help to guide them in a discussion. Therefore, the worksheet offers "hints" or ways to start the sentence at each skill. Of course, these are optional as they may not fit in each circumstance.

Discuss or role play several situations with the child and caregiver, or children. The therapist can use vignettes, or the child or caregiver can suggest real-life situations from home or school.

Suggestions to The Therapist

If the child or caregiver propose a situation from home or school, make sure it is not an emotionally laden one as these can be counterproductive in the learning process. Ask them to name a situation that is mild or neutral.

Role play a situation where the child is asking for what they need, and then another one where they are demanding in the request. Ask the child and caregiver to describe both experiences.

DEAR

Choose one situation to practice the skills; describe it below.

DESCRIBE OR SUMMARIZE THE SITUATION.
(*Hint: "Today . . ." or "When . . ."*)

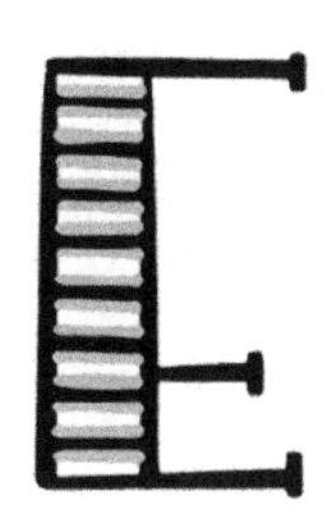

EXPRESS YOUR FEELINGS AND OPINIONS ABOUT THE SITUATION
(*Hint: "I am feeling . . ." and "I think . . ."*)

ASSERT YOURSELF BY ASKING FOR WHAT YOU WANT OR NEED, OR SAYING "NO" WHEN IT'S NEEDED
(*Hint: "What I need is . . ." or "No, I can't . . ."*)

REINFORCE OR REWARD THE PERSON AHEAD OF TIME
(*Hint: "I think it will help me/you/the situation because . . ."*)

Adapted from Linehan, DBT Skills Training Manual, 2015 (b)

4. CHEERLEADING

Cheerleading is a validation strategy. Children use cheerleading when they believe a situation is hopeless, it will never end, or that they cannot handle it.

Cheerleading is communicated by the therapist or caregiver to the child, and also by the child to him or herself. In the beginning, the therapist or caregiver actively cheerleads the child. As the child increases their self-validation, the therapist or caregiver reduces their frequency of validating comments to the child.

"In the beginning, the therapist or care-giver actively cheerleads the child."

Cheerleading helps to resist feelings of hopelessness, and feeling overwhelmed. In cheerleading, a child silently talks to him or herself just as they would to a friend, or in a way they would like people to talk to them in upsetting situations. The goal is to reduce negative self beliefs, and increase positive ones resulting in increased hope and confidence. As the therapist cheerleads, they offer the child reassurance and convey the belief that the child is doing the best they can in the situation. Children can create cheerleading comments from reflecting on the following ideas.

-Name my strengths that will help me get through the situation, ie; smart, nice, brave.

-Encourage myself to keep going. Things tend to improve in the future when kids stay the course.

-Remembering I have overcome similar situations in the past, and I can do it again.

A few examples of cheerleading comments are:

"Keep going; don't give up!"

"Stay strong and be brave!"

"I've got this!"

Handout Directions

Describe the cheerleading skill with the child and caregiver. Explain the goal of the skill and name future situations where it could be helpful to them. Discuss the three ideas listed above to consider as they create cheerleading comments. They can write these comments down on paper or in a note on their phone, and look at them during stressful life situations.

Discussion Questions

- What are a few of your strengths? (If child can not name any strengths, ask the caregiver to name a few. The therapist can add some too. By the way, this is cheerleading!)
- What are stressful situations you have overcome in the past?
- Is it easier to comfort yourself or others?
- Use the skill, cope ahead, to plan for future times when you may need to cheerlead yourself during stressful situations.
- What is a comment that will encourage you to keep going even when it is hard to do so?

Cheerleading

Self-Encouragement

Cheerleading is encouraging myself when I feel overwhelmed or hopeless. It helps me feel reassured, and strong enough to take on challenges. When I am cheerleading, I silently say a comforting comment to myself. . . just like what I would say to a friend.

I can create cheerleading comments by:

- Name my strengths that will help me get through the situation, ie; smart, nice, brave.
- Encourage myself to keep going. Things tend to improve in the future when kids are determined and hang in there.
- Remember I have overcome similar situations in the past, and I can do it again.

Examples of cheerleading comments are:
"Keep going; don't give up!"
"I finished my math paper yesterday; I can finish this one too!"
"I can do this!"
"I will be okay."
"I am brave!"

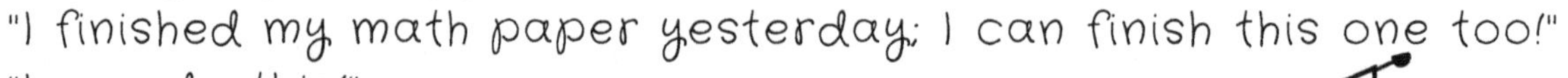

Adapted from Linehan, *DBT Skills Training Manual* (2015b)

Worksheet Directions

This sheet can be given for homework. It is important to use this one in session too, especially for a child who will need a lot of shaping to effectively cheerlead him or herself. Once the child has generated a list of cheerleading comments, role play the child facing a stressful situation and behaving skillfully.

Suggestions for The Therapist

The therapist will explain to the child that she may need to repeat the cheerleading comment to herself, over and over, until the stress subsides.

In the role play, the therapist or caregiver may first need to model cheerleading for the child, and then actively cheerlead the child in the role play.

Cheerleading

Self-Encouragement

Use the following questions to create encouraging comments for yourself during or prior to a stressful situation. Write your answers below.

1. What are my strengths that will help me get through this situation? (Some examples are: loyal, strong, brave, caring, smart, helpful, nice.)

2. Things tend to improve in the future when I am determined and hang in there. What words or phrases can I repeat to encourage myself to keep going?

3. I have overcome similar situations in the past, and I can do it again! What phrase or word can I say to remind myself of my past accomplishments?

Adapted from Linehan, DBT Skills Training Manual, 2015 (b)

SECTION 6

Caregiver Skills

This last section of the book describes several caregiver skills. As previously mentioned, children can be raised by many different people including: parents or step parents, foster parents, grandparents, aunt or uncles, or other relatives. On occasion, children are also being raised by friends of the family, or in a group home or residential care placement. As a result, the book will refer to all possible people raising the child as "caregiver." This section will describe skills for caregivers to implement with children.

The concept of dialectics, or the synthesis of two opposites, is a foundation in DBT. A dialectical tension is displayed in this section through the balance of change and acceptance strategies. Caregivers, like therapists, need to find the cadence of balancing the acceptance of their child while pushing them to make changes. This delicate balance from the caregiver helps to push the child to make changes in their behavior and choices while also showing them understanding and compassion through acceptance.

Weighing too heavily on one side or the other is confusing and frustrating for children. If the caregiver relies too much on acceptance the child may not see a reason to change or may push the limits with greater force. On the other hand, if the parent remains focused on change the child may feel invalidated and misunderstood.

This section will describe strategies of both acceptance and change. They will include acceptance strategies of validation, wise minded parenting, and relationship mindfulness. The change strategies are shaping, behavior charts, and ways to increase or decrease behavior.

ACCEPTANCE AND CHANGE STRATEGIES

1. VALIDATION

Validation is conveying to the child that they are being heard and understood. There is an interaction between the child and caregiver in the process of validation. When the caregiver validates the child it allows her to settle; she feels understood and accepted. Because the child feels heard, she feels free to express herself and therefore she is easier to understand, thus the caregiver validates her more.

This transaction can also go in a much different direction. When a child feels invalidated, they feel misunderstood and disregarded. As a result, they feel more vulnerable, their emotions become more intense and they behave with less control. The caregiver becomes more frustrated and less forgiving with the child, thus their invalidation increases. This leads to even more vulnerability on the child's part, and they show even less emotional and behavioral control.

It is important to note that often well-meaning caregivers inadvertently invalidate their child. This can occur through seemingly innocuous comments such as, "Don't worry" and "It'll be fine." Both of these transactions can become a habitual cycle in a family. Over time, the cycle becomes a dysfunctional dynamic within the family system. When caregivers are more aware of the cycle, they can interrupt it and work on creating a new cycle between themselves and their child.

Validation is highlighting what is valid and effective in a situation, it is not simply agreeing with anything the child says or does. Dr. Linehan (2015b) describes six levels of validation.

1. Pay attention- In this first level of validation, caregivers are showing open-minded listening and observing. They are fully engaged and paying attention to the child. Caregivers are setting aside their computer, tablet, show, and putting their eyes and ears only on the child in that moment.

2. Reflect back without judgment- The caregiver is reflecting back, or mirroring, what they hear and understand the child to be communicating to them. In this level of validation be careful not to reflect back word for word to the child as this can come across as mocking or parroting.

3. Read minds- In this third level of validation the caregiver is naming

the child's unverbalized emotion, thought, or behavior. The caregiver conveys this is an empathetic way with the intention of helping the child to clarify his or her own experience. The caregiver's comment is based on observations of the child's face, body language, or behavior. After making a validation based on mind reading, the caregiver will need to check in to make sure they are accurate. For example they could say, "Is that correct?' or "Did I get that right?"

4. Communicate an understanding of the causes. The caregiver validates that the child's behavior is understandable given previous events in the child's life. In level four, the caregiver can validate the child's learning from previous experiences (scared of a gerbil because one bit him), a previous event (two friends were invited to a classmates house and the child was not invited), and a mental or physical disorder (the child is scared to be away from the parent due to her separation anxiety).

5. Acknowledge the valid. In level five, the caregiver validates a child because their experience fits the present facts or because their behavior is reasonable in the current situation. An example would be the caregiver saying to the child, "Anybody would feel like that in this situation."

6. Show equality. In this level six validation, the caregiver shows respect and radical genuineness to the child. The caregiver shows the child they genuinely care about them, and they do not treat them as fragile. In this level the caregiver stays focused on the child, and when appropriate, matches the child's level of disclosure and vulnerability.

Handout Directions

Explain the concepts of validation and invalidation, and the six levels of validation to the caregiver.

Discussion Questions

- Describe a time when you felt validated and invalidated. Encourage caregivers to share their examples, and how each experience felt for them.
- What are the hardest times to validate your child? How can you behave skillfully in these moments?
- What do you think about this DBT saying? A child must feel accepted before he or she can change.

Validation

for Caregivers, pg. 1

Validation is expressing to your child that you are listening to them; and their feelings, thoughts, or behaviors are okay and make sense to you. Examples include comments such as, "I understand you're sad we couldn't go see grandma this week" and "It makes sense to me that you miss Bear; he's been our family pet since you were a little boy."

On the other hand, **invalidation** conveys to the child that their feelings, behavior, or thoughts are not okay; or that they are over reacting or are ridiculous. A few examples are mocking, eye rolling, sighing, ignoring; and comments like, "What's wrong with you? It's not that big of a deal" and "You just need to calm down."

The 6 Levels of Validation

1.Pay attention- In this first level of validation, caregivers are showing open-minded listening and observing. They are fully engaged and paying attention to the child. For example, caregivers set aside their computer, tablet, show, and put their eyes and ears only on the child in that moment.

2. Reflect back without judgment- The caregiver is reflects back, or mirrors what they hear and understand the child to be communicating to them. In this level of validation, be careful not to reflect back word for word as this can come across to the child that you are mocking them.

Adapted from Linehan, *DBT Skills Training Manual* (2015b)

Validation

for Caregivers, pg. 2

3. Read minds- In this third level of validation the caregiver is naming the child's unverbalized emotion, thought, or behavior. The caregiver communicates this in an empathetic way, and their intention is to help the child clarify his or her own experience. The caregiver can make a comment based on an observation of the child's face, body language, or behavior. After validating based on mind reading, the caregiver will need to check in to make sure they are accurate. For example the caregiver might say, "Is that correct?' or "Did I get that right?"

4. Communicate an understanding of the causes- The caregiver validates the child's behavior as understandable given previous events in the child's history. In level four, the caregiver can validate on the child's learning from a previous experience (scared of a gerbil because one bit him), a previous event (two friends were invited to a classmates house and the child was not invited), or from a mental or physical disorder (the child is scared to be away from the parent due to her separation anxiety).

5. Acknowledge the valid in the present circumstance- In level five, the caregiver validates because the child's experience fits the present facts, or because their behavior is reasonable in the current situation. An example would be the caregiver saying to the child, "Anybody would feel that way in this situation."

6. Show equality and radical genuineness- In level six validation, the caregiver shows respect and radical genuineness to the child. The caregiver is showing the child they genuinely care about them, are not treating them as fragile, and are matching their vulnerability. As an example, the caregiver might say, "I'm sad we argued before you left for school this morning too."

Worksheet Directions

This worksheet assists the caregiver in creating validating statements. Read each vignette and ask the caregiver to form one to two validations based on the six levels of validation. As the caregiver is learning to validate the child, the therapist will model validation for them. After the caregiver writes their validating statements, ask them to say the statements aloud or role play them with you.

Suggestions for The Therapist

It is vital for the caregiver to practice validating the child during the learning process. Look for opportunities for the caregiver to practice validating the child during each visit; prompt them to validate the child in session.

Remind the caregiver to validate only the valid. Validation is a powerful way to reinforce the child's behavior and words. Therefore, caregivers need to be careful when they are reinforcing the child.

Therapists can share these sentence starters for caregivers to use as they learn to create validating comments. A few are:

"It makes sense to me . . . "

"It sounds like you're saying . . . "

"What I hear you saying is . . . "

Validation

for Caregivers

Following each vignette below, write 1 -2 validations based on the six levels of validation.

1. Your son comes home from school complaining he has no friends. He isn't crying, but his eyes are teary. You ask what happened and he states, "No one plays with me at recess. They don't let me on a team."

Validation:

Validation:

2. Your foster child shares that she misses her birth mom, and hasn't seen her in over a year. She turns away from you, and gets very quiet.

Validation:

Validation:

3. Your granddaughter doesn't like to clean . . . anything. Her room is an absolute mess, and you can't avoid it any longer. You ask her to clean her room; she stomps her feet , growls, and yells "You're the worst nana ever!"

Validation:

Validation:

Adapted from Linehan, *DBT Skills Training Manual* (2015b)

2. RELATIONAL MINDFULNESS

In relational mindfulness, the caregiver pays attention to the child in the moment, and in a nonjudgmental and effective way. When caregivers are mindful in the relationship, they are better able to regulate their own emotions and are less reactive to the child.

As caregivers practice relational mindfulness, they are increasingly able to notice their own thoughts and judgments. This allows caregivers the opportunity to let go of any need to change or fix things, and instead just be mindfully present with their child. The mindfulness HOW and WHAT skills are inherent in relationship mindfulness (Fruzzetti 2006). Let's look at each of them.

"When caregivers are mindful in the relationship, they are better able to regulate their own emotions and are less reactive to the child."

Observe- Notice your child; pay attention to his or her action, comment, body posture, facial expression, and tone of voice.

Describe- Describe the observable things that your child is doing without interpretations or judgments.

Participate- Actively be in the moment with your child; let go of being self-conscious and fully participate in activities.

Nonjudgmental- Remain in a nonjudgmental stance with your child. Avoid judgments of good/bad, right/wrong, or should/shouldn't which lead to invalidation and a disconnected relationship. Instead, stick with facts and name your observations.

One-mindful- Do not multi-task when you are spending time with your child. Be in the current moment, doing one thing at a time.

Effective- Let go of being "right" or seeking revenge with your child. Do what works to meet your relationship goals with your child, and do not let your emotions get you off track.

Handout Directions

Describe the skills of relational mindfulness that are based on the HOW and WHAT skills. During the discussion, practitioners will take their time so that caregivers can share their own experiences. These examples will be valuable as practitioners explain the skills.

Discussion Questions

- Typically, what gets in the way of being fully present with your child?
- Do you ever get stuck in being "right" or seeking revenge with your child?
- What skills can you use to manage judging thoughts or behaviors?
- What are your relationship goals with your child?

RELATIONAL MINDFULNESS

for Caregivers

Relational mindfulness is fully paying attention to your child in the moment, and in a nonjudgmental, effective way. The skills of relational mindfulness are:

Observe- Notice your child; pay attention to his or her actions, comments, body posture, facial expression, and tone of voice.

Describe- Describe the observable things that you notice about your child or what he or she is doing, without interpretations or judgments.

Participate- Actively be in the moment with your child; let go of being self-conscious.

Nonjudgmental- Remain in a nonjudgmental stance with your child. Avoid judgments of good/bad, right/wrong, or should/shouldn't which lead to invalidation and disconnected relationships. Instead, stick with facts and name your observations.

One-mindful- Don't multi-task when you are spending time with your child. Be in the current moment, doing one thing at a time.

Effective- Let go of being "right" or seeking revenge with your child. Do what works to meet your relationship goals with your child; don't let your emotions get you off track.

Adapted from Fruzzetti, *The High-Conflict Couple* (2006)

Worksheet Directions

This worksheet will be given as a homework assignment, and it will also be used in session to practice relational mindfulness with the caregiver. Discuss a situation that may typically occur between the caregiver and child, and ask the caregiver to describe his or her answer to each of the relational mindfulness skills. The therapist can also role play a situation with the caregiver, and then ask them to describe each skill.

Suggestions for The Therapist

Relational mindfulness covers several skills, and initially, it is a lot for caregivers to bear in mind. At first. the therapist may choose one skill, or choose only the WHAT or HOW skills to learn and practice.

Initially, the caregiver may be hesitant to share their judgmental or revengeful thoughts or behaviors, or their stance of being "right" in the relationship with their child. Once they do disclose them, it is important for the therapist to remain nonjudgmental and validate their bravery in sharing this information.

RELATIONAL MINDFULNESS

for Caregivers

Practice relational mindfulness with your child.

Observe- I pay attention to my child's actions, comments, body posture, facial expression, and tone of voice.

Describe- What I noticed about my child (no interpretations) is:

Participate- Did I actively stay in the moment even during times of distraction or self-consciousness?

Nonjudgmental- Did I have any judgmental thoughts or behaviors? Was I able to change them to facts or observations? Describe them.

One-mindful- Was I in the current moment, doing one thing at a time with my child? Describe it.

Effective- My relationship goals with my child are:

Did I let go of being "right" and seeking revenge?
(I will not let my emotions get me off track!)

Adapted from Fruzzetti, *The High-Conflict Couple* (2006)

3. WISE MIND PARENTING

There are three states of mind which includes: emotion mind, reasonable or thinking mind, and wise mind. Emotion mind is ruled by feelings and urges. In emotion mind, it is hard for caregivers to think logically, and their decisions are influenced by their emotions.

Reasonable mind is ruled by facts and logic. In reasonable mind, the caregiver ignores feelings and empathy, and would prefer to be practical when problem solving with their child.

Wise mind is a blending or synthesis of both reason and emotion, and is the wisdom within each person. In wise mind, the caregiver blends emotion and reason, and is willing to accept reality even when they do not agree with it. In wise mind, caregivers are clear-thinking, calm, compassionate for themselves and their child, centered, and courageous. Following are a few examples of the three states of mind for caregivers.

Emotion mind- Excessive worry about your child; engaging in a back and forth, yelling match with your child; rushing in to "fix" a problem for your child; and saying shaming comments to your child when you are feeling overwhelmed.

Reasonable mind- Using only logic to discuss problems with your child, moving forward from an argument with your child without resolving hurt feelings, responding to your child's emotions with a stoic facial expression, having a "whatever" attitude when your child is emotional.

Wise mind- Choosing not to argue about a small issue because your relationship with your child is more important, bringing up an emotionally sensitive subject with your child at a later time when you both are calm, remaining calm and validating your child even though her voice is angry and her words are rude, staying focused on your relationship goals with your child even during tense moments.

In Dr. Kastner's (2013) *Wise Minded Parenting* there are numerous wise mind parenting mantras. The following ones are adapted from *Wise Minded Parenting*, and are helpful for parents to repeat to themselves during challenging situations.

- In order to help my child change, I must first accept her or him unconditionally.

- My love messages really matter, even if my child can't resist showing me irritation and rudeness.
- I may be right, but it is effective to insist on my opinion right now?
- I won't give in to unwanted behaviors just to get the situation to end.
- My child is doing the best she can given her emotional sensitivity.

Note: There is only a handout for this skill.

Handout Directions

Describe the three states of mind with caregivers. Next, take turns reading the wise mind parenting mantras adapted from Dr. Kastner's work (2013). These mantras usually initiate discussion among caregivers as many relate to the messages within each mantra. Allow caregivers to contribute to the conversation as much as they feel comfortable and safe to share.

Discussion Questions

- Do you tend to get stuck more often in emotion or reasonable mind?
- Which "C" words will help you to identify being in wise mind?
- Do you disagree with any of these mantras? Explain your answer.
- Which of the mantras is the most challenging to accept? Which is most helpful?

Suggestions for The Therapist

Ask the caregiver to choose one or two wise mind parenting mantras to say to themselves over the week. Suggest that the caregivers take a picture of the mantras, and place it as wallpaper on their phone or computer to see on a daily basis.

Wise Mind Parenting

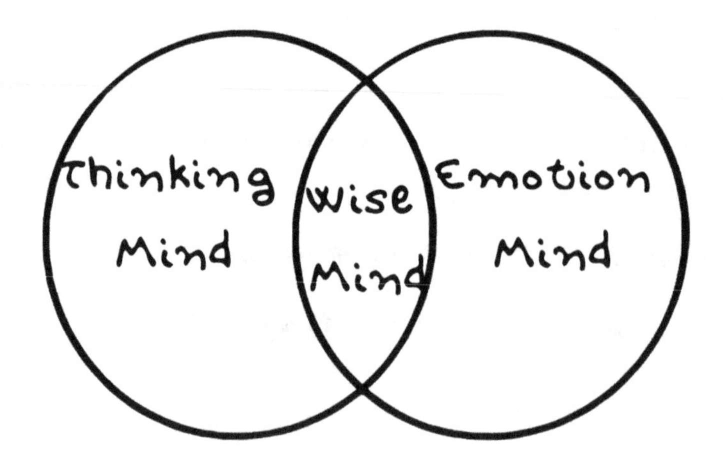

In emotion mind, you may excessively worry about your child; engage in back and forth, yelling matches; rush in to "fix" problems for your child; and say shaming comments when you're feeling overwhelmed.

In thinking or reasonable mind, you may only use logic to discuss problems with your child; move forward from an argument without resolving hurt feelings; respond to your child's emotions with a stoic facial expression; and have a "whatever" attitude when your child is emotional.

In wise mind, you may choose not to argue about a small issue because your relationship with your child is more important; bring up an emotionally sensitive subjects at a later time when you both are calm; remain calm and validate your child even though her voice is angry and her words are rude; and stay focused on your relationship goals even during tense moments.

Wise Mind Parenting Statements

- In order to help my child change, I must first accept her/him unconditionally.
- My love messages really matter, even if my child can't resist showing me irritation and rudeness.
- I may be right, but it is effective to insist on my opinion right now?
- I won't give in to unwanted behaviors just to end the situation.
- My child is doing the best she can given her innate emotional sensitivity.

Adapted from Kastner, *Wise Minded Parenting* (2013)

4. SHAPING BEHAVIOR

Most of the time, behavior change takes time and is a slow process. Shaping is a positive reinforcement strategy that increases a child's desired behaviors. Shaping is used with complicated behaviors that require more than one step, or in evoking desired behaviors that the child does not already display.

Shaping is reinforcing small, successive steps of new behavior to reach a larger goal. Caregivers identify a larger goal, and then break it down into smaller steps (A -Z). As the child completes the first smaller step (A), the caregiver reinforces the behavior. They continue to reinforce this first behavior until it occurs on a consistent basis.

Next, the caregiver increases the child's requirement to two behaviors (A and B). Once the child completes the two behaviors, the caregiver reinforces both of these behaviors.

The caregiver continues to slowly increase the requirement (A, B, and C) in order for the child to earn the reinforcer. This continues until the child reaches the larger goal.

Handout Directions

Describe the behavior change skill, shaping. Use the example of 8-year-old Anna and her mother, Karla, from the handout to further explain the skill. Therapists can also explain the skill with a neutral subject such as completing a recipe or a DIY home project.

Discussion Questions

- Caregivers, what are some of your own behaviors that you would like to change that involve multiple steps?

SHAPING

for Caregivers

Shaping is reinforcing small, consecutive steps of a new behavior in order to reach a larger goal. In shaping, the caregiver identifies a larger goal, and then breaks it down into smaller steps (A - Z). When the child completes the first small step (A), the caregiver reinforces the behavior. The caregiver continues to reinforce this first behavior until it occurs on a consistent basis.

Next, the caregiver asks the child to do two behaviors (A and B). When the child completes the two behaviors, the caregiver reinforces the child.

The caregiver slowly increases the requirement (A, B, and C) in order for the child to earn the reinforcer or reward. This continues until the child reaches the larger goal.

Following is the example of 8 year old, Anna, and her mom, Karla which correlates to the figure below. Karla's larger goal is for Anna to clean her bedroom. The initial step (A) is for Anna to pick up her clothes off the floor; Karla reinforces this behavior with her smile, a "thank you," and a star on Anna's chart.

When Anna picks her clothes up consistently, Karla adds the next step— make the bed. Then, when Anna picks up her clothes (A) and makes her bed (B), Karla reinforces these behaviors. Karla continues to add new steps until Anna consistently cleans her whole bedroom (the larger goal).

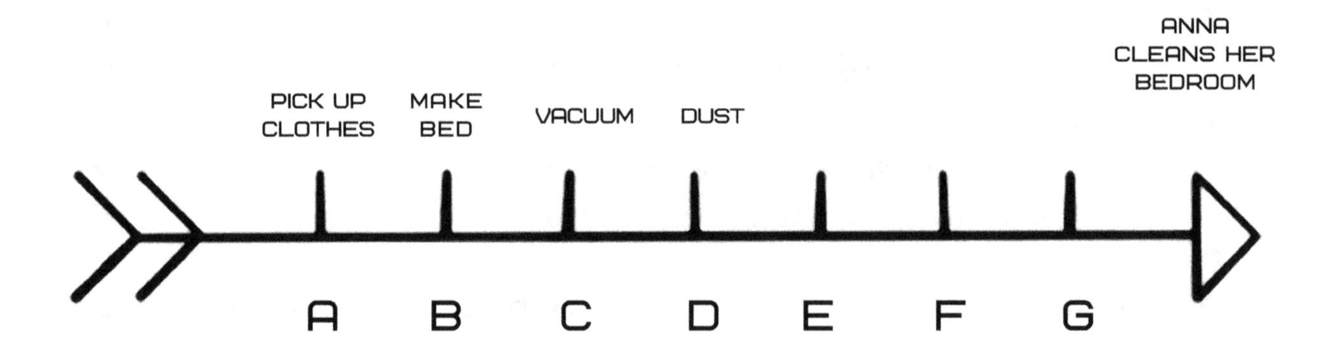

Adapted from Linehan, *DBT Skills Training Manual* (2015b)

Worksheet Directions

The worksheet is given to caregivers as homework, and it is also used as practice in session. The more practice the caregiver has in session, the more likely they are to use skillful behavior at home. Continue to explain the concept of shaping from the handout discussion. In session, therapists can use additional vignette examples, or examples mentioned by the caregiver.

Suggestions for The Therapist

Inform caregivers that timing with a reinforcer is important. It is more effective to positively reinforce the child immediately after they show the desired behavior. If caregivers wait too long to reinforce behavior, the reward and behavior are no longer connected, and thus the reward loses its influence.

SHAPING

for Caregivers

LARGER GOAL:

SMALLER STEPS TO GOAL

A:

B:

C:

D:

E:

F:

G:

LARGER GOAL:

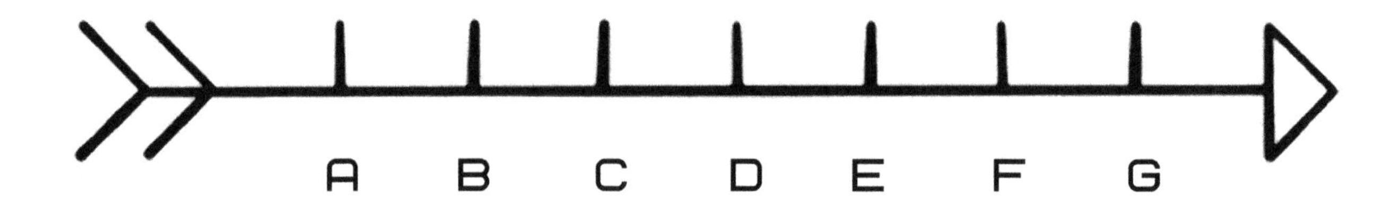

Adapted from Linehan, *DBT Skills Training Manual* (2015b)

5. BEHAVIOR CHART

Behavior charts are a fun way to motivate kids and increase desired behaviors. Children are more interested when caregivers make the chart fun, and like a game. Caregivers can personalize the chart by adding pictures related to the reward or to the child's interests; they can also put playful and lively stickers on the chart.

Choose from one to three behaviors. Define the desired behaviors clearly and specifically, stating what you *want the child to do* instead of what not to do. As an example instead of saying, "Don't yell," say, "Use a soft voice inside the house."

"Define the desired behaviors clearly and specifically, stating what you want the child to do instead of what not to do."

Decide how often to reinforce the behavior, for example, once a day at bedtime or twice a day at lunch and bedtime. At the designated time (lunch, bedtime) fill in a square for each desired behavior the child has shown during the time period. Once the child has completed all of the open spaces and reaches the end of the game board on the chart, they earn the stated reward.

Before the caregiver and child begin the chart they: review the goals, discuss rewards the child would like to earn, decide on a reward, and write the reward on the chart. Find rewards that are desirable and otherwise unattainable so that the child will be motivated by them. Choose rewards that only cost a few dollars, and that are relationship based such as, go on a bike ride with mom. Change the chart frequently to maintain your child's interest as they quickly get bored with the same chart.

Note: There is only a worksheet for this skill.

Worksheet Directions

There are two behavior charts included in this section. They are both weekly charts with seven open spaces though they can be altered by the caregiver. For example, a caregiver may create a chart with only three open spaces for the child to complete.

As stated above, caregivers will decide on the goals and number of spaces needed to complete the chart. The caregiver will discuss this with the child, and together they will identify a reward. At the designated time, the caregiver will fill in (with stickers, bingo daubers, a check mark, or Xs) the open space if the child has completed the desired behavior as stated in the goal.

The caregiver and child use the behavior chart during the week. Once the chart is completed, the child will redeem it for a reward, and then bring it to the session to show the practitioner. Then, the caregiver will begin a new chart.

Discussion Questions

- What are the top 1-3 behaviors you would like to work on with your child?
- Goals are to be stated with a clear, specific description of the desired (*what you do want to see*) behavior. Change the following goals to clear, specific descriptions of desired behavior.

    1. My child needs to stop yelling.
    2. I want my child to quit whining and complaining all the time.
    3. I'm tired of my child avoiding his homework every night.
    4. I want my child to stop hitting her brothers and sisters every time she doesn't get her way.

Suggestions for The Therapist

Caregivers can use the charts as templates and change the goals, rewards, and the required number of open spaces to completion. They can write from 1 to 3 goals, and choose a different reward for each chart. When there are too many open spaces on the chart for the given week, caregivers can fill in spaces by adding game or cheerleading comments such as: move ahead, skip a space, keep going, you've got this, yay, way to go, stay strong, and be brave! Have fun and be creative with the charts.

Behavior Chart for:

GOALS:

1.

2.

3.

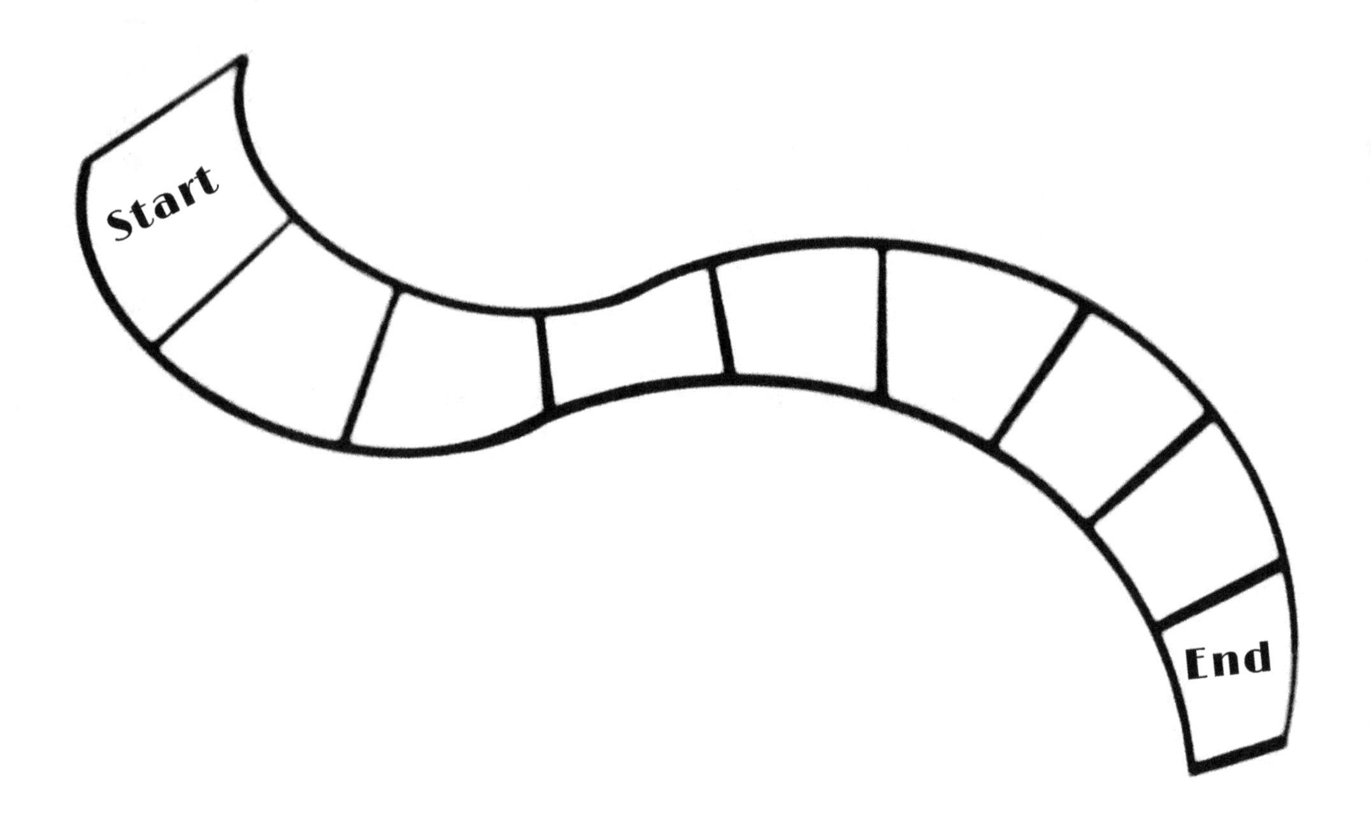

When ____ squares are filled in, you will EARN:

Behavior Chart for:

GOALS:

1.

2.

3.

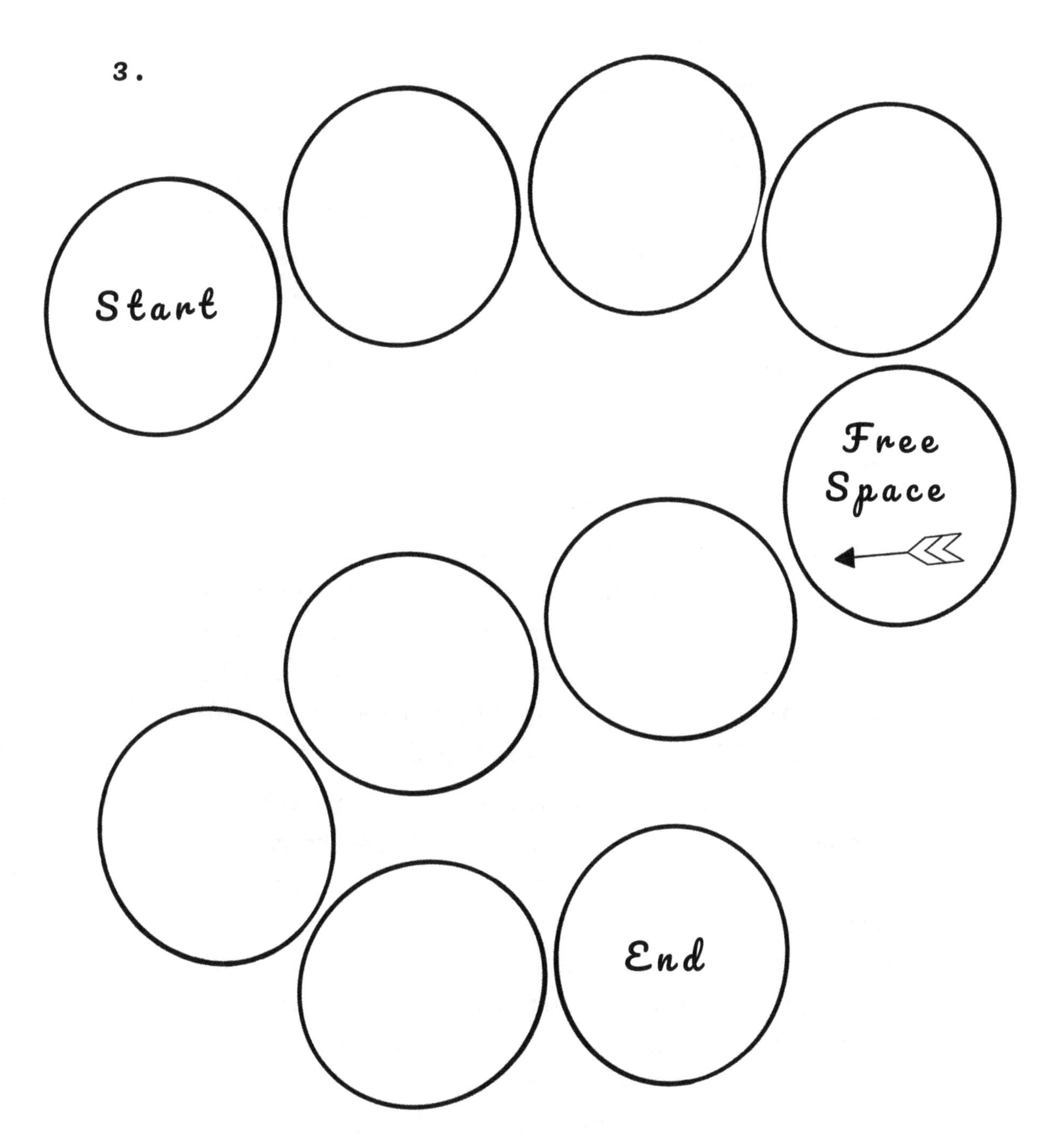

When ____ circles are filled in, you will EARN:

6. INCREASE AND DECREASE BEHAVIOR

Caregivers need to understand behavior change strategies in order to be effective as they help their child to make behavior changes. Let's discuss ways to increase or decrease behavior and relevant strategies.

Increase Behavior

Strategies to increase the possibility of a behavior are accomplished through *positive reinforcement*. A *reinforcer* is any positive consequence that increases the possibility that a behavior will happen again. A positive consequence, or reward, is anything that the child likes or values such as, time with friends and family, food or candy, attention, and participating in a hobby or craft. The reward is only as powerful as the child's interest in it, and for example, if the child does not like to play video games they will not influence her behavior. The following are some additional thoughts on reinforcement with children.

- Timing of the reinforcement is important; it needs to happen immediately following the desired behavior. When a reinforcer occurs much later than the behavior, it is not as influential.
- A caregiver's reinforcement is negated when they combine it with criticism or other invalidation. One example is a mom asking her child to sit up and discuss a current problem. The child turns over while still laying down but does maintain eye contact, and the caregiver says, "Okay, thanks, Paige. Now come on, sit up; you're too old for this! Don't you want to be a big girl?"
- Sometimes parents inadvertently reinforce an unwanted behavior. For example, negative behaviors are reinforced when the caregiver pays attention to them. Caregivers must remember to deliberately *ignore* a behavior they do not want and *attend* to a behavior they do want. As an example, a dad feels his eight-year-old son "should" already be able to turn in his completed homework. When the boy does turn in his homework, his dad does not mention it. On the other hand, when his son forgets to turn it in, dad gives the behavior loads of negative attention saying, "Why didn't you turn it in? I got a call from your teacher and you've got missing assignments . . . again!"
- Catch them being good! Pay attention to the positive choices of the child, even if it only lasts for a short period of time. For example,

as soon as caregiver notices it they can say, "Thanks for showing me eye contact!"

Decrease Behavior

Now, let's look at ways to decrease undesired behavior. *Extinction* is decreasing a problem behavior by discontinuing the reinforcement of it. One example of this is foster mom, Janice wants to reduce her son's screaming. When Jason screams, Janice ignores the behavior; over time he will stop the screaming behavior.

Caregivers need to be aware of the *behavioral burst*. When a behavior has been reinforced and the reinforcement stops, there will be a temporary increase in the problem behavior. If the caregiver continues to stop the reinforcement, the problem behavior will eventually decrease. For example, Janice ignores Jason's screaming. Initially, Jason screams more and louder. Janice stands firm in ignoring it and over time, Jason's screaming happens less and less at home.

"Caregivers need to be aware of the behavioral burst."

Another strategy to decrease behavior is *punishment* which occurs when caregivers add a consequence to the problem behavior. The consequence is either adding something negative such as time-out, or taking away something positive like an upcoming family outing. Over time, punishment is a less effective strategy for behavior change while reinforcement is experienced as more effective.

Natural consequences are another type of effective punishment. At times, caregivers may not be able to find a natural consequence for a problem behavior, or the situation could be dangerous. A natural consequence for the child who does not complete homework is to allow the child go to school with incomplete work. Another example is a child who refuses to brush her teeth. Caregivers allow her to go to school with unbrushed teeth and face peers who comment that her teeth look stained. Of course, on paper these sound easier than they are in life! If the caregiver plans to allow the natural consequence, they need to be careful not to interrupt the situation and inadvertently reinforce the wrong behavior.

Handout Directions

Describe the strategies to increase and decrease behavior. Pay attention to the many definitions on the page, and spend extra time defining each new word. Write them on a white board for caregivers to see.

Discussion Questions

- Define each of the following behavior change strategies, and give an example for each one: reinforcer, positive consequence, extinction, behavioral burst, punishment, consequence, and natural consequences.
- Do you agree with the statement, Rewards are only as powerful as the child's interest in it? Explain your answer.
- When a caregiver follows reinforcement with criticism or invalidation it negates the effect of the reinforcement. Can you give an example of this?
- When a caregiver decreases a problem behavior through extinction they will likely experience a behavioral burst. Have you ever experienced a behavioral burst with your child, and how did you stand strong to get through the behavioral burst until the problem behavior decreased?
- Can you give an example of a consequence that adds something negative, and one that takes away something positive?
- Provide an example of a time you used natural consequences with your child.

Increase & Decrease Behavior *for Caregivers*

INCREASE BEHAVIOR

Positive reinforcement strategies increase the likelihood of a behavior.

A **reinforcer** is any positive consequence that increases the probability that a behavior will happen again.

A **positive consequence**, or reward, is anything that the child likes or values, such as time with friends.

Rewards are only as powerful as the child's interest in it.

The reinforcement needs to happen immediately following the desired behavior.

A caregiver's reinforcement of the child is negated when they combine it with criticism or other invalidation.

Caregivers can inadvertently reinforce an unwanted behavior. Caregivers must remember to deliberately ignore or punish a behavior they do not want and attend to a behavior they want.

Catch the child being good! Pay attention to the positive choices of the child, even if it only lasts for a short period of time.

DECREASE BEHAVIOR

Extinction is decreasing a problem behavior by discontinuing the reinforcement of it.

Be aware of the **behavioral burst.** When a behavior has been reinforced and the reinforcement stops, there will be a temporary increase in the problem behavior. If the caregiver continues to stop the reinforcement, the problem behavior will eventually decrease.

Another strategy to decrease behavior is **punishment** which occurs when caregivers add a consequence to the problem behavior.

A **consequence** is either adding something negative such as time-out, or taking away something positive like an upcoming family outing.

Over time, punishment is a less effective strategy for behavior change while reinforcement is experienced as more effective.

Natural consequences are another type of effective punishment. Caregivers may not be able to find a natural consequence for a problem behavior, or the situation may be too dangerous to allow the child in it.

Adapted from Linehan, *DBT Skills Training Manual* (2015b)

Worksheet Directions

This is another worksheet with two purposes; it can be used for continued skill strengthening in session, and also as a homework assignment for skill generalization.

Suggestions For The Therapist

There is a lot of potential new information on these pages. It is advisable to check in with caregivers to determine if the information is familiar or new to them. When the information is new, therapists may divide it into two parts teaching strategies to increase behavior in one session and strategies to decrease it in another.

Caregivers may believe that punishment needs to be extreme in order for it to be effective. In fact, it does not need to be extreme and is more effective when it is clear, specific, and time limited.

Increase & Decrease Behavior *for Caregivers*

INCREASE BEHAVIOR

Name positive behaviors that your child did over the week . . . even small ones:

DECREASE BEHAVIOR

Name 1 - 3 unwanted behaviors that you would like your child to decrease over the week:

Name the situations when you reinforced your child over the week:

Identify specific behaviors you wanted to increase in each situation:

Identify the specific reinforcers you used to increase the above behaviors:

What did you observe was the outcome of your reinforcement?

Name the situation and behaviors you ignored:

What did you observe was the outcome of ignoring the behaviors?

Name the situation and consequences (adding a negative, taking away a positive, or allowing a natural consequence) to decrease unwanted behaviors:

What did you observe was the outcome of the consequences?

Adapted from Linehan, *DBT Skills Training Manual* (2015b)

REFERENCES

Burrows, L. (Winter 2011). *Relational Mindfulness in Education.* ENCOUNTER: Education for Meaning and Social Justice, 24(4): 1-6.

Hooker, K.E., Fodor, I.E. (2008). *Teaching Mindfulness to Children.* Gestalt Review, 12(1): 75-91.

Fruzzetti, A. (2006). *The High-Conflict Couple: Dialectical Behavior Guide to Finding Peace, Intimacy & Validation.* Oakland, CA: New Harbinger Publications.

Kastner, L. (2013). *Wise Minded Parenting: 7 Essentials for Raising Successful Tweens + Teens.* Seattle, WA: ParentMap.

Linehan, M.M. (2015a) *DBT Skills Training Handouts and Worksheets,* 2nd edition. New York: The Guilford Press.

Linehan, M.M. (2015b) *DBT Skills Training Manual, 2nd edition.* New York: The Guilford Press.

Linehan, M.M. (1993) *Cognitive-Behavioral Treatment of Borderline Personality Disorder.* New York: The Guilford Press.

Lozier, C. (2018) *DBT Therapeutic Activity Ideas for Working With Teens.* London: Jessica Kingsley Publishers.

Mazza, J.J., Dexter-Mazza, E.T., Miller, A.L., Rathus, J.H., and Murphy, H.E. (2016) *DBT Skills in Schools: Skills Training for Emotional Problem Solving for Adolescents (DBT STEPS-A).* New York: The Guilford Press.

Moonshine, C. (2008) *Acquiring Competency and Achieving Proficiency with Dialectical Behavior Therapy, Volume II: The Worksheets.* Eau Claire, WI: PESI Healthcare.

Perepletchikova, F., Axelrod, S. R., Kaufman, J., Rounsaville, B. J., Douglas-Palumberi, H., & Miller, A. L. (2011). Adapting dialectical behaviour therapy for children: Towards a new research agenda for pediatric suicidal and non-suicidal self-injurious behaviors. *Child and Adolescent Mental Health, 16,* 116 -121.

Rathus, J.H. and Miller, A.L. (2015) *DBT Skills Manual for Adolescents.* New York: The Guilford Press.

AUTHOR BIO

Carol Lozier MSW LCSW is an author and psychotherapist. She is a clinical social worker in private practice in Louisville, Kentucky. Ms. Lozier has spent over thirty years counseling children, teens, and adults in the issues of trauma, and adoption and foster care. Ms. Lozier is an intensively trained DBT therapist.

Ms. Lozier has published four books, and contributed articles to two parenting books. Her most recent book is *DBT Therapeutic Activity Ideas for Working with Teens* (2018). Contact Ms. Lozier on her website www.carollozierlcsw.com.

CPSIA information can be obtained
at www.ICGtesting.com
Printed in the USA
LVHW050458200621
690630LV00003B/18